A PRIMER IN FAMILY THERAPY

A PRIMER IN FAMILY THERAPY

By

WILLIAM M. WALSH, Ph.D.

Chairman, Department of Counselor Education
Northeastern Illinois University
Chicago, Illinois

CHARLES C THOMAS • PUBLISHER

Springfield • Illinois • U.S.A.

Published and Distributed Throughout the World by

CHARLES C THOMAS • PUBLISHER
Bannerstone House
301-327 East Lawrence Avenue, Springfield, Illinois, U.S.A.

ISBN 0-398-03992-5

Library of Congress Catalog Card Number: 79-21010

With THOMAS BOOKS *careful attention is given to all details of manufacturing and design. It is the Publisher's desire to present books that are satisfactory as to their physical qualities and artistic possibilities and appropriate for their particular use.* THOMAS BOOKS *will be true to those laws of quality that assure a good name and good will.*

Printed in the United States of America
V-R-1

Library of Congress Cataloging in Publication Data

Walsh, William M
A primer in family therapy.

Bibliography: p. 125
Includes index.
1. Family psychotherapy. I. Elkun, Leonard D., joint author. II. Title.
RC488.5.W35 616.8'915 79-21010
ISBN 0-398-03992-5

To my loving family:
Kathleen
Karen
Kristen

THEORY OF PERSONALITY

All happy families are alike, but an unhappy family is unhappy after its own fashion.

Leo Tolstoy
Anna Karenina
1877

THERAPEUTIC PROCESS

I could explain what is wrong with you, but in psychology an explanation does not constitute a cure.

Lawrence Duvell
French author, poet, dramatist
1968

INTRODUCTION

COUNSELING, as a helping process, is not new or modern. It can be traced to the very roots of civilization. Many of the famous people of ancient and modern history performed therapeutic functions in their own unique way. Other helpers, indeed the vast majority, were unknown, simple people: teachers, friends, relatives, and associates of troubled contemporaries. Only recently has the concept of interpersonal helping relationships been formalized into an academic discipline or science. The field of psychotherapy and counseling is a twentieth century phenomenon. In the early days, eighty years ago or so, therapy was rather narrowly restricted to individual contact in private consultation rooms. Pioneer practitioners, such as Freud, Adler, Jung, and the early behaviorists, developed their ideas in their daily practice and in rather crude laboratory settings. In some instances, they attempted to apply the scientific method borrowed from the physical sciences. They wanted to describe, classify, and quantify their observations in a systematic controlled fashion. The results of their labors were the first, rigorously organized theories of human behavior. Over the years, from then to now, their work has been analyzed, expanded, rejected, and gradually incorporated into several dozen major theories of therapy. To say that psychotherapy and counseling is a major feature of modern society would not, I believe, be an overstatement. Therapists, today, have something to say about and considerable influence upon almost every aspect of contemporary animal and human life.

During the past several decades, counseling has considerably broadened its perspective. No longer do therapists work exclusively on a one-to-one basis with clients. Multiple counselor, multiple client, and small group arrangements are relatively common in almost every counseling setting. Today, a new model may be added to this listing: Family Counseling. Counselors, in increasing numbers, are replacing or supplementing their traditional individual and group models with a family oriented approach. When I say that family therapy is new, it is so in a relative sense. The term *family counseling* is really not new. Early practitioners recognized the need for some contact with a client's family. However, the focus of their therapeutic interventions was still the intrapsychic processes of the individual. They may have been interested in the effect that intimate family members had on the patient in question, but the locus of change was still in the individual. What is new is the current definition of the term.

Today, family counseling refers to a specific way of conceptualizing human problems and actualizing treatment procedures. Rather than focusing on intrapsychic processes, the family therapist looks to interpersonal variables as the source of difficulty in the individual. A person may be experiencing considerable difficulty in functioning, but the origin of the problem does not reside in him. It is outside of him in his family and social network. The individual, in fact, may be a victim of his interpersonal network and carry the symptoms for the entire system. It is not uncommon to see, in family therapy, one person dysfunctioning for the entire family. The family looks to be functional and controlled, while one individual is defined as being maladaptive. In other situations, the dysfunction is more widespread and the entire family appears to be pathological. Regardless of how the situation appears at first glance or how the family defines its difficulties, the family therapist looks for pathology in the interpersonal processes of the unit. Hence, the intrapsychic versus the interpersonal orientation is the major differentiating factor between family therapy and all other modes of counseling intervention.

Within the narrow field of family counseling there are a number of acceptable models of therapy. There is by no means a consensus on how to do family therapy, or no one prescribed way to practice family counseling. The past twenty-five years have seen the development of several major approaches to working with families. One of the earliest and still most popular approaches is the "Communication model." The original work that forms the basis of this theory was developed in the early 1950s in Palo Alto, California. A research project directed by Gregory Bateson studied the relationship of interpersonal communication and schizophrenic behavior. His coworkers in the project were Jay Haley, John Weakland, and Donald Jackson. This diverse team of researchers and clinicians gradually developed the core concepts of this model. In 1959, Virginia Satir joined this group and in the next several years the seminal ideas were formalized into a cohesive theory of family therapy. All of the original theorists gradually went their separate ways and began spreading their ideas to other parts of the country. Today, Jackson, Haley, and Satir are the primary spokesmen for the Communication model of family therapy.

Another major model of family therapy began in the early 1950s, but at the other end of the country from California. At Georgetown University in Washington, D.C., Murray Bowen continued the work with families that he had begun several years before in Topeka, Kansas. His work also focused on schizophrenic patients and their families. Using general systems theory, he developed a unique therapy model with several original concepts. His conceptualizations of family triangles, undifferentiated ego mass, multigenerational transmission process, and emotional cut-off have stood the test of time and critical evaluation. Today they form the basis for his Systems model of family therapy.

In the mid years of the 1960s, two other models of family therapy developed from previous concepts of individual and family therapy. They are the Structural model of Salvador Minuchin and the Social Learning Approach of Gerald Patterson. Working with families referred to the Philadelphia Child Guidance Clinic, Minuchin focused on the structure of the family as the prime variable in functional and dysfunctional families. In the past dozen years, he has developed one of the most comprehensive treatment models in the family therapy field. His treatment interventions are frequently original, aggressive, intrusive, and dramatic. Gerald Patterson, on the other hand, has applied standard behavioral principles to the treatment of families. Using operant conditioning techniques, he has produced quick and efficient change in disturbed families. His research has shown the effectiveness of this model, particularly with families who have behaviorally disturbed children.

The final theoretical model covered in this text is Integrative Family Therapy. It is my own personal framework that developed from my clinical training and experience. The title *Integrative Family Therapy* is, I believe, an accurate description of the focus of the theory. Basically, it is an integration of several components into one consistent model. First, it is an integration of the ideas of other family theorists with my own personal background. Specific ideas and techniques have been selected from other models and modified to fit my philosophy and personality. Second, it is an integration of these selected concepts of family therapy with the traditional ideas of individual personality development. A practitioner of this approach may follow any one of the many intrapsychic models of therapy and combine those with the major propositions and techniques of Integrative Family Therapy.

From the beginning of the family therapy movement, several decades ago, psychoanalysis has had an impact on the development of theoretical models. Many of the early theorists had psychoanalytic training, and portions of this theory can be seen in their own family therapy models. Leonard Elkun, a psychoanalyst, has been interested for several years in the relationship between these two schools of therapy. His chapter, Family Therapy and Psychoanalysis, provides an enlightening comparison between family therapy and psychoanalysis and points out the many similarites between the two in basic theory and practice.

The four major theoretical approaches, my presentation of Integrative Family Therapy, and the discussion of Family Therapy and Psychoanalysis by Leonard Elkun are the contents of this text. It is my belief that these six chapters represent the major theoretical emphases in the field today. They are not intended to be an all inclusive coverage of a specialty area. Many other theorists have made major contributions to the development of family therapy. Individuals like Nathan Ackerman, Carl Whitaker, Lyman Wynne, Theodore Lidz, and David Mendel, to name a few, are widely known and respected.

However, for an introductory exploration of any new area, there must be a starting point. The chapters in this text, in my opinion, present a diverse introductory overview of the field of family therapy. The serious student will of course go beyond this presentation and eventually cover the full range of thinking in the field. For the uninitiated in family work, this is the place to begin.

Organization of the Text

This text is intended for use as an introductory book in the field of family therapy. It can be used as an independent reader for the practitioner or as a required text in an introductory course. Since it is a primer, a first reader, it is structured to cover the greatest volume of material in the shortest, least complex format. Each chapter is organized in the same manner, so that similarities and differences are readily apparent. The reader can compare and contrast several treatment procedures, for instance, without a great deal of reading and searching. A professor can structure his class presentations based on the consistent format of each chapter. In short, the sections and subsections of each chapter are designed to facilitate the acquisition of new material in a concise, coherent manner.

The first section of each chapter is a brief description of the major theorist(s) for that particular model. Their major publications are listed so that the reader may seek out the original source material of the theory and study each model in greater depth. The second section provides the background for the theory. The next section, Theory of Personality, is devoted to the theoretical formulations of each model. This section expresses the theorists' conceptualizations of human behavior. It attempts to provide explanations for functional and dysfunctional behavior. The final section of each chapter is devoted to a presentation of the therapeutic process. In each case, specific steps in therapy are identified and specific techniques are described. The final two sections of each chapter are followed by a list of key works and phrases. These are intended to serve as a review of each theory and a study guide for the individual who wishes to check his own comprehension of the material.

CONTENTS

A PRIMER IN FAMILY THERAPY

CHAPTER 1

COMMUNICATION MODEL

DESCRIPTION OF MAJOR THEORISTS

DONALD JACKSON, M.D.

PROFESSIONAL POSITIONS. Founder, Mental Research Institute, Palo Alto, California. Psychiatrist, Veterans Administration Hospital, Palo Alto, California.

MAJOR PUBLICATIONS. *Communication, Family, and Marriage.* Palo Alto, Science and Behavior, 1968. *The Etiology of Schizophrenia.* New York, Basic Books, 1960.

JAY HALEY

PROFESSIONAL POSITIONS. Clinical Professor of Psychiatry, University of Maryland. Director, Family Therapy Institute in Washington, D.C.

MAJOR PUBLICATIONS. *Problem-Solving Therapy.* San Francisco, Jossey-Bass, 1976. *Changing Families: A Family Therapy Reader.* New York, Grune and Stratton, 1971. *Strategies of Psychotherapy.* New York, Grune and Stratton, 1963.

VIRGINIA SATIR

PROFESSIONAL POSITIONS. Past Director, Esalen Institute, Big Sur California. Past Director of Training, Mental Research Institute, Palo Alto, California.

MAJOR PUBLICATIONS. *Peoplemaking.* Palo Alto, Science and Behavior, 1972. *Conjoint Family Therapy.* Palo Alto, Science and Behavior, 1967.

INTRODUCTION TO THEORY

THE Communication model in family therapy was one of the pioneering attempts to treat disturbed individuals within the context of their family unit. As we have already seen, the initial work of the original Palo Alto group

(Bateson, Jackson, Haley, Weakland) led to formal research projects, workshops, and clinical applications related specifically to treating families. When Jackson founded the Mental Research Institute, joined by Haley and Satir, the Communication model soon became a national influence in psychotherapy circles in general and a leader in the family therapy movement.

In reality, the Communication model is a collection of slightly different treatment philosophies that share a common core belief. The core belief is that human communication is the most important characteristic of family life. Clear honest communication between family members promotes the mutual resolution of problems and conflicts and is expressed in a pleasureable family life style. Dysfunctional communication, on the other hand, directly produces tension in the family unit. This tension may be expressed in a number of ways, one of the most common being emotional disturbances in one or more family members.

Beginning with this common core of beliefs, the various Communication theorists have developed their own unique conceptualizations of functional and dysfunctional communication processes and their own treatment strategies. This chapter is devoted to the ideas of three of those theorists: Jackson, Haley, and Satir. Jackson is included because of the universal acceptance of two propositions concerning family communication for which he is largely responsible: family homeostasis and double-bind communication. Even though he did not promulgate a comprehensive theory of family therapy, his ideas have affected the thinking of most family theorists to the present day. Haley and Satir have developed comprehensive frameworks of family therapy, and they are presented as the two prime examples of the communication model.

THEORY OF PERSONALITY

Donald Jackson

Doctor Jackson's contributions to the early development of a family therapy approach have had a significant impact on almost every model of therapy in the past twenty-five years. He never really established a Jacksonian theory that is distinct from other therapy models. Rather, his ideas are so well accepted that they are incorporated into every theory since that time. The two major ideas that have gained widest acceptance and that have had the most impact are his explanation of the dynamics of family homeostasis and his development of the concept of double-bind communication.

Family homeostasis is the term that he uses to describe the balance seeking process that he observed in the families of schizophrenic patients. These families had considerable difficulty resolving conflicts in their unit, and this inhibited their ability to solve long-range and short-term problems. They also had a strong desire to have peaceful harmonious relationships. Jackson saw this peaceful state resulting from a balance of a family's perceived needs and their eventual satisfaction. Lack of need satisfaction would lead to imbalance and create tension in the unit. This tension-filled unbalanced state is undesirable and is to be avoided at any cost.

The desire for balance is universal in families. Healthy, functional families seek alternate ways when their need satisfaction is blocked or frustrated. They are sufficiently open and creative to devise new strategies for handling current problems. Dysfunctional families do not have the means to seek alternatives for tension reduction. They have the same desire for peace and balance, but are frustrated in achieving it because of inadequate problem-solving methods. Hence, they develop unhealthy methods for reducing the tension in their unit. One of the most common methods is to project the tension onto one family member, who then becomes the symptom bearer or sick one. The family can then focus their attention on the sick one and, in effect, avoid dealing with the real source of the tension and conflict. By taking the tension out of the unit and placing it on one individual, they create balance or homeostasis in the family. Since tension throws the system out of balance, whenever a conflict occurs the sick one will receive the tension and balance will be restored in the rest of the members. The sick one is frequently referred to as the "scapegoat," since the unit is in a sense sacrificing him for the good of the whole. The schizophrenic patient is viewed as the scapegoat in his family.

He is the recipient of the tension that is present in an unhealthy family.

The process that creates balance in the family has been referred to as the "homeostatic mechanism." Whenever tension rises to an unacceptable level and the system is unbalanced, the homeostatic mechanism will be triggered and the unit will come back into a state of homeostasis. Viewed from this perspective, the homeostatic mechanism is dysfunctional and must be countered in therapy. In unhealthy families, the mechanism is in constant force and the result is a severely disturbed individual. However, the homeostatic mechanism can be in operation in well-adjusted families, but may not be as constant or pervasive. In other words, all families seek balance in their unit and all will use homeostatic mechanism at one time or another.

The second concept that has gained wide acceptance is the notion of double-bind communication. Jackson's development of this concept grew directly out of his work with the Palo Alto research group and his treatment of schizophrenic patients at a VA hospital. The original members of the research group, Bateson, Haley, and Weakland, formally developed the hypothesis of double-bind communication patterns. Jackson, working as the psychiatric consultant to this group, related the idea to his therapeutic work and expanded it to the point of being a major concept in his view of the development of schizophrenic behavior.

Double-bind communication patterns involve at least two people. One of the parties is the scapegoat or victim. The second person is the sender of a double message. The victim is receiving two conflicting messages from the sender. On the one hand, he receives a positive statement from the sender. For instance, a mother may tell her son that his behavior in a specific situation is good and he should be proud of it. On the other hand, the victim is receiving a contrary message negating the positive feeling. The mother may be nonverbally communicating annoyance, disappointment, or unhappiness about the boy's behavior. The victim has thus received two conflicting messages, and he doesn't know which one to respond to or to believe. If he responds to the first message and feels good about his behavior, he is risking the possibility of annoying or disappointing his mother. If he responds to the second message he may seek to change his behavior, but he is confused about her interpretation of good and bad. In other words, he is damned if he does and damned if he doesn't.

The double-bind messages are repeated over a period of time and constitute a pattern of confused communications. The victim may continue to repeat the behavior in order to find some meaning in it. Is it good or bad, acceptable or unacceptable? In reality, there isn't one meaning, and it is a futile search. After years of repeated double-bind messages, the victim develops one or more unhealthy responses. He may continue to search for meaning in a double meaning situation and become increasing more frustrated. He may attempt to respond to each part of the double message, hence find meaning in neither. This futile search can lead to a personal philosophy of meaninglessness and general view of all communication as being senseless and worthless. The victims third alternative is to withdraw from the situation in order to block the meaningless material. He escapes from the situation by shutting out all communication from the sender. In its extreme form, this constitutes psychotic withdrawl by shutting out all communication from the world.

Jackson considered double-bind communication to be a prime factor in creating schizophrenic behavior, but he also saw it present in less severely disturbed families. He eventually identified several necessary conditions that are present in all double-bind situations:

1. The presence of two or more people in a communication network. One of these people is the victim.
2. The double-bind communications must be repeated over a period of time, constituting an habitual pattern.
3. One of the messages must be perceived as a negative statement. For example, a mother tells her child not to stay after school and play with the other boys. Or, she may tell him to play with other children under the threat of punishment. The punishment can take a variety of forms: anger, withdrawl of love, or physical abuse, to name a few.
4. The second message is usually on an abstract level and

contradicts the first message. This one is also enforced by punishment. It can be a verbal or a nonverbal communication. Using the previous example, the mothers secondary message would be, "You should have more friends and if you don't....." The secondary message could also be given by the other parent.

5. The individual feels trapped in the situation because of the family bond. There are no alternate ways of responding open to them except for the unhealthy responses mentioned previously.
6. After a period of time, all of the five elements do not have to be present. The victim has developed a response set to the world based on double-bind communications, and any one part of the process can trigger the conditioned response of the individual.

In dysfunctional families these double-bind patterns are firmly established and highly resistant to modification. In most cases, the family is unaware of the unhealthy process, and it must be dramatically brought to their awareness. The goal in counseling is for the therapist to interrupt the process and help the family to begin sending clear single messages. Since the old patterns are habitual, the new, clear communications need to be repeated many times in order to change the victim's unhealthy response.

Jay Haley

Over the years, Haley has taken the basic communication concepts of personality developed in Palo Alto and adapted them to his own personal style in therapy. Since his conceptions of personality development are similar to the other communication theorists that are covered in this chapter, only those ideas of his that are unique or different will be discussed in this section.

Haley is primarily concerned with a family's communication patterns and their resulting personal alliances. The relatively stable patterns that people develop directly influence the way they behave among themselves and with outsiders to the family. The family groupings that inevitably occur are a result of the patterns that are used to meet needs and to solve problems. In a healthy family, the communication patterns and the individual alliances will be such that allow for mutually satisfying need fulfillment. The dysfunctional family, on the other hand, can be characterized by confused patterns and unstable alliances.

According to Haley, functional communication follows an orderly sequence that eventually transmits accurate information. That is to say, one statement follows another in a progressive fashion in order to communicate a total idea or feeling. Disturbed communication patterns have confused sequences and therefore transmit inaccurate information. This confusion and inaccuracy can lead to misinterpertations, assumptions, and misunderstandings among family members. If family members do not know each other's needs and expectations, they can hardly be expected to fulfill them in any reasonable manner. This lack of need fulfillment produces stress and conflict in the unit.

In the family unit, there is a hierarchy of relationships that helps to channel communication in the most productive direction. A natural hierarchy in many families is provided by the generational distinction between the members. In an extended family, for instance, the grandparents may constitute the upper level of authority and control in the family. The parents would reside in the next highest level and the children in the lowest level. In nuclear families, the parents may be the top level in the hierarchy with the lower levels being occupied by the children in chronological order by age.

Stress and conflict can result in a family when the hierarchy is not clearly understood by each member. Alliances that cross hierarchial levels can also cause stress and conflict. In either case, individuals may not know where they stand in relation to others when issues of authority, control, or decision-making are present. In one situation, a child may be praised for accepting parental responsibility and in the same situation at a different time be punished for parenting a younger child. One parent and a grandparent can form an unhealthy alliance against the other parent. Parents and children frequently group together against another family faction. Any combination of individuals in alliances is possible and potentially healthy in the family.

However, the lack of clarity and consistency in hierarchical relationships can be a central problem in dysfunctional families. In order to change the maladaptive behavior of individuals in a family, the therapist must work to effect a change in the family situation that is causing and supporting the behavior. To do this, he focuses on the communication patterns and the alliances that are present in the family unit.

Virginia Satir

Virginia Satir is the most widely known spokeswoman for the communication model of family therapy. From her original work with the Palo Alto group, she has developed her ideas into a comprehensive theory of personality and theory of therapy. This theory incorporates the ideas of other theorists, but also contains many unique elements that are strictly Satir. She has effectively disseminated these ideas internationally through her writings, teaching, and speaking engagements. Since her theory is well-developed and comprehensive, this discussion will be limited to an overview of the major concepts and prime elements of the theory of personality.

Satir considers the family unit to be one part of the total social environment that contains it. Stresses and strains in the total environment will thus affect the specific family. The individual family member is an integral part of his unit and is affected by events in that smaller system. There exists, then, a transmission process of cause and effect from the society to the family to the individual. An individual member's behavior cannot be fully understood without also considering these larger units. A change in one of these larger systems will ultimately affect the behavior of every small part of those systems. Hence an individual's dysfunction, or "pain" as Satir prefers to call it, is symptomatic of dysfunction or pain in one of the larger units. Symptoms expressed in one family member are often an expression of trouble in the entire family. In this context, symptoms are purposeful and descriptive of more complex and widespread difficulties.

A family, while grappling with a troubled situation, may attempt to find fault with or place blame on one member. Satir calls this person the *identified patient* (IP). Families frequently contact a therapist with complaints about a specific IP. The problem may be more pervasive, but the family is telescoping it onto one person and labeling that individual as disturbed. The term *identified patient* is important then, as referring to the families' identification of the individual and not the therapists' interpretation. The therapist will take a much broader view of the symptomatic behavior.

Satir believes that the key factor in both functional and dysfunctional relationships is communication. It is a complex process that involves both the giving and the receiving of verbal and nonverbal messages. Clear communication is essential in order to give clear messages to others. It is also necessary, obviously, to receive clear messages from others. Connotations, abstractions, overgeneralizations, and assumptions are prime examples of unclear communication methods. These faulty communication patterns breed dysfunction in a family and are then transmitted to an individual member. The individual is in sense being victimized by poor communication methods in the entire family. Homeostasis in the unit is more crucial than individual stability. The imbalance caused by unresolved con-

TYPICAL SEQUENCE OF EVENTS

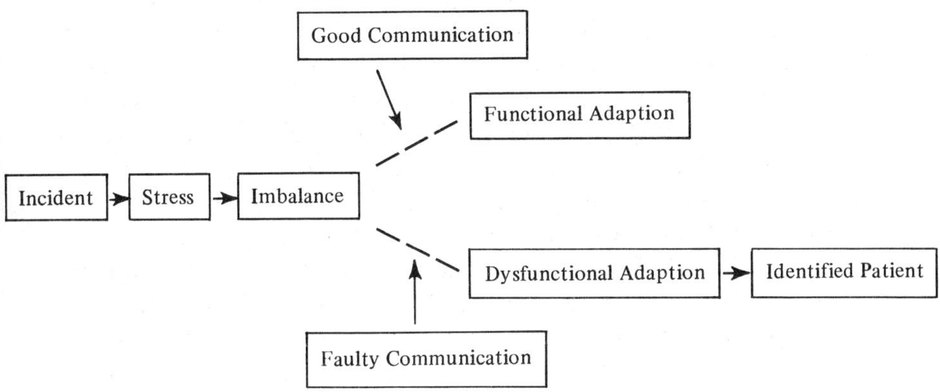

Structure 1

flict must be righted at the expense of one of the family members. The person's symptoms serve the purpose of regaining balance in the system. The victimization may not be purposeful or consciously pursued, but the result is rather systematic and predictable. A typical sequence of events in a problem situation can be depicted as illustrated in Structure 1.

The sequence begins with an incident between family members or between the family and the outside world. This incident causes stress in the unit and unbalances the delicate homeostasis that exists. Some resolution of the incident must be achieved in order to lower the stress and balance the system. A healthy family will use good communication methods in order to achieve a functional resolution of the conflict. An unhealthy family, lacking effective communication methods, will not resolve the incident in a functional way. Lacking this resolution they must then transmit the stress to the identified patient. This individual will eventually develop symptoms, and he will carry the dysfunction for the entire family. The crucial point in this sequence of events is the attempted resolution of a problem using either good or faulty communication methods. Faulty methods lead directly to dysfunction, which is expressed in the IP. Therefore, the remediation of individual problem behavior is focused entirely on the family communication process.

The origin of poor communication methods is in the parental relationship. The two people may have each learned faulty methods in their families, and they continue to use them in their relationship. As children grow, they learn how to communicate from their parents. From infancy, all of us are taught the patterns that allow us to interact with the world. If there are faulty patterns in the family, it is likely that one or more children will also develop communication problems. The development of effective patterns requires the guidance of mature individuals. A mature person has learned how to communicate all aspects of himself, intellectual, emotional, and physical, to others. He knows how to satisy his own needs with the help of others and how to help other individuals satisfy their personal needs. He can act responsibly in the world because he has learned to communicate properly. Defenses are minimal since there is little threat to his personal security. The dysfunctional individual has not learned how to effectively interact with others, and he may be considered immature and underdeveloped in interpersonal relationships.

One of the most important factors in an effective communication process is congruency. An individual's perception of an event should be accurate and should have a strong basis in reality. A primary source of dysfunction in individuals and families is an inaccurate perception of a situation that distorts the way they view and interact with the world around them. Difficulty accepting differentness in ourselves and others is another stumbling block to the development of effective communication. Parents who depreciate a child because of the development of different characteristics or behaviors are creating the basis for self-doubt and insecurity. As he grows, any display of differentness on the part of others can be perceived as threatening to his already weak self-concept. He may feel, "If this person is right and I believe differently, I am wrong and less of a person." This attitude can lead to a rigid approach to the world or a rejection of others through withdrawal.

Dysfunctional families have learned faulty communication processes. As we have seen, they learn them in order to reduce the stress in their family and to achieve a homeostatic state. One of the most common ways for a family to reduce stress is to assign specific roles to individual members and to have them acted out in the conflict situation. Dysfunctional families usually develop inappropriate roles for their members. Satir identifies three frequently played roles that are used by dysfunctional families to reduce stress. These roles cannot be played alone. They must be used in some combination to avoid conflict. For instance, a blamer must have a placator so that the interaction will reduce stress. The three dysfunctional roles are as follows:

1. *Placating* — attempting to avoid a conflict situation by being overly agreeable or giving-in to another person. Nonassertive, passive, accepted behavoir is the norm. This

person is sometimes referred to as the martyr in a relationship.

2. *Blaming* — avoidance of conflict by increasing the stress temporarily and forcing the other person into a passive-defensive position. A person in this role will overreact in an aggressive way in order to protect a weak personal position on a particular issue or to guard a poor self-concept. Acting out behavior may be part of the blaming role. It may also be seen as a power play in a relationship.
3. *Irrelevancy* — this role is an attempt to reduce stress by avoiding the conflict situation. This person distracts the other participant(s) from the conflict. By shifting the focus from the immediate conflict situation, confrontation is avoided and stress is temporarily reduced. Common irrelevant behaviors include psychosomatic illness, inappropriate talking or playing in a counseling session, abrupt changes in the topic of conversation, and temper tantrums.

Since these roles are all faulty methods of communication, they are an excellent focal point for intervention by the therapist. The counselor will attempt to have the participants switch to a more appropriate role. Satir calls this fourth role "congruency." Congruent communication involves the direct relating of what is happening intellectually, emotionally, and physically at that time by each participant in the relationship. Dysfunctional families display little direct, realistic communication. By developing this role for each family member, the therapist is providing the most powerful tool for permanent change in the whole unit. The essence of this change is reflected in the behavior of each family member by their increased ability to resolve conflicts and to solve problems in the future.

Key Words and Phrases

Family homeostasis
Double-bind communication
Dysfunctional family
Homeostatic mechanism
Individual "pain"
Identified patient
Family communication
Problem sequence

Scapegoat	Faulty communication
Communication sequences	Differentness
Hierarchy of relationships	Dysfunctional roles
Family alliances	Congruent communication

THERAPEUTIC PROCESS

Jay Haley

Haley conceives of the therapeutic process as brief and intense. The focus is on the resolution of specific problem situations that are presented by the family or that are observed by the therapist. As the family changes to deal with the present difficulties, it changes its structure and pattern of communication. This change in the present can be permanent, and it can provide new strategies for meeting future conflicts. Since the process is brief, the therapist must be active and directive from the outset and assert control from the first session.

Haley identifies six steps in the therapeutic process. Theoretically, the steps occur in sequence and are spread over several sessions. However, because the process is short-lived, all of the steps may occur in the first session. They may all be repeated in successive sessions as needed. For example, the therapist might move sequentially from first introductions to direct intervention in the first session. The second session may also warrant some social interaction as a warm-up to more intense interactions later in the session. The therapist should allow for all of the stages to occur for as long as necessary with the realization that the final three are the most productive for problem solving.

The following are the six steps in the process:

1. *Social Stage* — therapist and family members meet and engage in superficial social-type exchanges. In the first session, the therapist may use this time to explain his process to all of the family members. In succeeding sessions, this stage allows the participants a brief time to reorient themselves to the working parts of the session. During this time, the therapist can observe family members and interactions without focusing on threatening material.

2. *Problem stage* — therapist asks the family to explain the presenting problem. Usually, the parents begin the discussion, but all family members are given a chance to participate in the initial discussion. Frequently, it is the person who arranged for the counseling contact who makes the first effort at communicating the family distress.
3. *Interaction stage* — the therapist helps the family to elaborate on the presenting problem. He observes how family members interact with each other in a potentially stressful situation. He can note the emerging communication sequences, personal alliances, and family hierarchies. The therapist can remove himself somewhat from these interactions by instructing the family to exclude him from the conversation. He can then observe the process from a third person perspective. At times it may be instructive to have the family enact a problem situation and role play a real life conflict.
4. *Goal-setting stage* — therapist helps the family to define one or more specific goals for the immediate future. All members are encouraged to participate in this task, and considerable personal negotiation of individual commitment may result in the process. Mutual satisfaction with the goals, and a commitment to their attainment, is the therapeutic goal at this stage.
5. *Intervention plan* — therapist develops the plan of intervention strategies that he will use in succeeding sessions. This plan is based on hypotheses that he has developed from his observations and from the mutual goals of the family.
6. *Intervention* — therapist uses directives in order to involve himself more intensely with the family and to structure the family in the direction of change. The directives are new behaviors that family members will engage in. They may be rehearsed in the session, but they must be carried out in real life. The directives will be reviewed in the following sessions, and they can be changed or modified by mutual consent.

The therapy process is terminated when all family members and the therapist feel that the goals have been achieved. Theoretically, successful therapy has resulted in new communication patterns in the family that will help them to realize their future goals. This has been accomplished by the process of open communication, realistic goal-setting, and the development of new individual behaviors. The therapist has facilitated this process by being active, directive, and involved.

Virginia Satir

The major focus of therapy is to develop new methods of communication in the family. These new methods will ease the dysfunction in the identified patient. The therapist's role is to act as the "official observer" in the family and the professional consultant for the family system. At times, the counselor may be very active and overtly direct verbal and nonverbal communication. At other times, the therapist may take a nondirective stance and covertly influence the content and direction of the session. Satir believes that both types of counselor behaviors are appropriate with different families or with the same family at different times. Generally speaking, the more disorganized and dysfunctional family will need an aggressive limit-setting therapist. As the family develops more appropriate controlled interactions, the therapist can take a nondirective position. Individual family members are now more responsible for their behaviors, and they can communicate themselves directly to one another. As the family moves to higher levels of functioning, the therapist's active role is diminished and eventually ceases to be influential in day-to-day living.

In order to move a family to higher levels of functioning, Satir has developed a loosely organized therapeutic process. It is loosely organized in the sense that she does not adhere to rigidly defined stages that must be accomplished before change can occur. It is more of a free-flowing process that is structured by the therapist. The focus is constantly an awareness of the present moment. Are individual family members aware of their own and others' communication processes? Are they aware of the congruency and differentness present at this moment in themselves and others? Awareness is the thread that runs through the entire process. The therapist will directively or nondirectively structure the sessions in order to increase the possibilities for awareness. It is this structuring that gives the counseling process its form and organization.

Five interlocking and interwoven steps can be identified in the therapeutic process. The first step involves the establishment of trust in each other by all participants in the session. The therapist will stress the confidential nature of their relationship. He may take the lead by controlling the initial interactions of the participants. He wants to gain the family's confidence in his ability to help them remove their pain. Trust and confidence are necessary ingredients for later therapeutic interventions. As the family becomes more comfortable with counseling, the therapist will begin to focus on awareness activities. These activities are designed to use the family's own experiences to highlight problem areas.

One of the most effective awareness experiences that Satir advocates is the family-life chronology. It is essentially a question and answer process that explores the specifics of a family's history, their expectations of one another, and how they have chosen to meet their own and each other's needs. The chronology begins with questions about the family's past. The parents' own families are briefly discussed, and the therapist guides the exploration systematically into the present situation. The chronology provides a wealth of information for the therapist, but it also creates awareness in each family member. New information is frequently presented, and family interactions can be stimulated by nonthreatening material. The chronology is one way that the therapist can encourage active participation in all members. Other awareness experiences involve an exploration of a family's typical day, common home conflict situations, individual's roles in the family, and how each individual communicates certain messages to other members. All of these activities are keyed to the development of greater awareness by using the families own past experiences.

Based on the new awareness that results from a family's exploration of past and present experiences, the therapist creates new understandings in the family system. Reasons for certain behaviors or attitudes can be emphasized. "Whys" can be more clearly understood by all members. Based on these understandings, new modes of communication can be developed. When a family sees what is happening to them, they can create new behaviors to relieve the dysfunction. The final step in the process involves the application of these new behaviors in daily life. Trial and error and continued practice are to be expected and encouraged by the therapist. New interactions can be role-played in the sessions, and feedback to the participants can be modeled by the therapist. The therapy session can become a safe microcosm of everyday life.

The therapy process can be of short duration or may involve frequent sessions over many months. The critical factors determining length of therapy appear to be the degree of disorganization in a family, the amount of dysfunction recognized by the family, and the responsiveness of the system to the therapists interventions. The therapist should be sensitive to these factors and not be impatient when change is not immediately forthcoming.

Key Words and Phrases

Stages in process	Therapist's role
Directives	Nondirective behavior
Appropriate Termination	Family-life chronology
Steps in Process	Awareness activities

CHAPTER 2

SYSTEMS MODEL

DESCRIPTION OF MAJOR THEORIST

MURRAY BOWEN, M.D.

PROFESSIONAL POSITIONS. Director, Family Center of Georgetown University. Professor of Psychiatry, Georgetown University.

MAJOR PUBLICATIONS. The use of family theory in clinical practice. *Comprehensive Psychiatry, 7*:345-374, 1966. Family psychotherapy. *American Journal of Orthopsychiatry, 30*:40, 1961. *Family Therapy in Clinical Practice.* New York, Jason Aronson Publisher, 1978.

INTRODUCTION

MURRAY BOWEN was one of the first therapists to relate general systems theory, which he garnered from other disciplines, to the study of the family. He saw the family, both nuclear and extended, as a system much like other large scale systems, i.e. societies, large and small corporations, and organizations. They all function under the same principles, and their dysfunction can be understood in similar terms. When Bowen discusses the family as a system, he is also talking about larger and more complex entities.

Bowen began his professional career with training in the traditional psychoanalytic model. He used this methodology to treat severely disturbed individuals, particularly schizophrenics. Very early in his professional life, he saw more progress with his patients when the family was involved. Patients who were hospitalized experienced a quicker recovery and a more orderly transition back into society when their families were part of the treatment process. These insights gradually developed into a large research study at the National Institute for Mental Health in 1954. As part of the study, families lived with the patients in the hospital for short periods of time. They could all, then, be treated intensively by the staff involved in the study. Initially, the families were treated using traditional individual therapy methods. After a short period of time, the entire staff switched to a family approach. This family approach was based on psychoanalytic concepts exclusively. Bowen called his new methods "Family Group Therapy." Interest in this new field of investigation grew, and the number of research studies increased. More therapists were impressed with the new methods, and the therapy moved from an institutional setting exclusively to private outpatient settings.

As Bowen became more involved with his new treatment procedures, he began to develop new ideas for observing and diagnosing the problems he saw in families. From his initial focus exclusively on the mother-child relationship, he recognized the significant involvement of the father and other family members. Grandparents were included, and his ideas about the effects of illness in multiple generations began to take shape. The emotionality that he observed in disturbed families led to his investigation into the difference between thinking processes and statements, and feeling states and verbalizations.

Over a period of years, these new insights were gradually blended with the emerging concepts of general systems theory. The relationship patterns in the family were considered to be similar to other, larger relationship networks such as business and community organizations. His emphasis on the importance of systems theory was so considerable that his name has been linked with family systems ideas, and his theoretical approach became known as *Family Systems Theory.*

THEORY OF PERSONALITY

The family is a system. The basic system is comprised of individual members. These individuals do not function independently of one another, any more than the departments in a company operate autonomously. There is a central oneness that holds the individual parts together. Sometimes this feeling of oneness is unhealthy. This is particularly true when people are overdependent on one another. In a situation like this, uniqueness may be discouraged for the sake of togetherness. Bowen characterizes this quality as *stuck togetherness.* The more dependent individuality breeds dysfunction. It is difficult for individual members to differentiate themselves from each other. They are seen as undifferentiated parts of the total system. Stuck together individuals tolerate minimal input from outside of their unit, and they can quickly turn in on themselves in times of crisis.

Bowen subscribes to the basic principle of systems theory. That is, that a change in one part of the system affects all the other parts of the system. In fact, he used this principle as the key change agent in therapy. If one family member can begin to develop greater individuality, he can cause changes in the family that will reverberate throughout the entire system. The more undifferentiated a family is, the more difficult this is to accomplish. The system has an innate need to maintain the *status quo*. Thus the concept of homeostasis and balance is critical to an understanding of the system. Almost any behavior that maintains the homeostasis in the family will be tolerated. Even self-destructive behaviors are preferred over behaviors that will "upset the applecart."

In the process of adapting systems theory and psychoanalytic concepts to the field of family therapy, Bowen postulated eight interlocking concepts that explain in more specific terms the functioning of the family. The remainder of this discussion on personality theory is devoted to a presentation of these interlocking concepts.

Triangle

The triangle is the basic building block of the system. It is composed of three individuals, each one representing a side of the triangle. It is the smallest unit of the system and the progenerator of balance in the system. It represents the most stable pattern of relationships between individual members. Dyads, two person relationships, are seen as too unstable since they are not complex enough to handle stress or discomfort. Bowen believes that dyads will invariable seek a third component to form a triad, or triangle.

During calm periods, the triangle consists of a comfortably close twosome and a less comfortable third party. The parties in the twosome relate well to one another, and the third person seeks to intrude on that relationship. When things are calm in the system, the third person is not really needed to maintain the balance. In periods of stress, the third party is essential in order to disperse the tension and restore the desired balance. Therefore, the third person is tolerated in the relationship as an essential ingredient in time of need. When stress occurs between two people, they use the third person as the recipient of that projected tension. The tighter the triangle, the more the third person will feel the tension. The result is that the original twosome in the relationship rid themselves of tension and function more harmoniously. The third party is their stabilizing factor.

In tension states, the triangle typically has two comfortable sides and one side in conflict. As behavior patterns are repeated over a period of years, the members of the triangle develop fixed roles in relation to each other. The classic example of a family triangle is the father-mother-child relationship. When there is tension between the parents, they will project this onto the child. Instead of the parents arguing about a situation, the mother may find herself in conflict with her daughter. This frees the father from the original stressful relationship with his wife and allows them to commiserate about the poor mother-daughter relationship. Bowen calls this behavior the *family projection process*. This process may occur on a daily basis for a number of years. The topic of disagreement may change, but the pattern is always the same. Eventually, the child will develop symptoms and may be seen by the family as the disturbed one. Actually, the disturbance resides in the father-mother relationship and is untreatable as long as the triangle remains intact in its present form.

Families develop rather fixed patterns of triangles and as such they are identifiable and predictable. Each individual in the family may be involved in several triangles all of them interrelated in a family pattern. Nonfamily members may also be involved in triangular patterns within a family. This usually happens when the existing patterns are inadequate to manage the stress that is occurring. Individuals will reach out to others and bring them into the rigid patterns that are existent. It is not uncommon for therapists or social agencies to be triangled into an unhealthy family. The result is not therapeutic. In fact, an impasse in therapy may be the result of the therapist being triangled in and effecting a reduction of tension. Stress is reduced in this case, but change has not occurred. When therapy is terminated, the family will continue its dysfunctional behaviors.

The triangle is thus the primary element in the system. Individual behaviors can be understood in terms of the triadic concept, and therapeutic maneuvers can be designed to change patterns and configurations. The therapist must, however, remain outside of the system if he is to effect any lasting reorganization and change.

Differentiation of Self Scale

Bowen developed the differentiation of self scale as a way of measuring and describing the amount of individuality in a family. The scale is a way of expressing the amount of stuck togetherness that exists in the system. Generally speaking, the more differentiation that individuals exhibit, the less dependence there is in the system and the more flexible are the triangular patterns. It is essential, therefore, to assess each persons level of differentiation in order to gain a thorough understanding of each family's system.

DIFFERENTIATION OF SELF SCALE

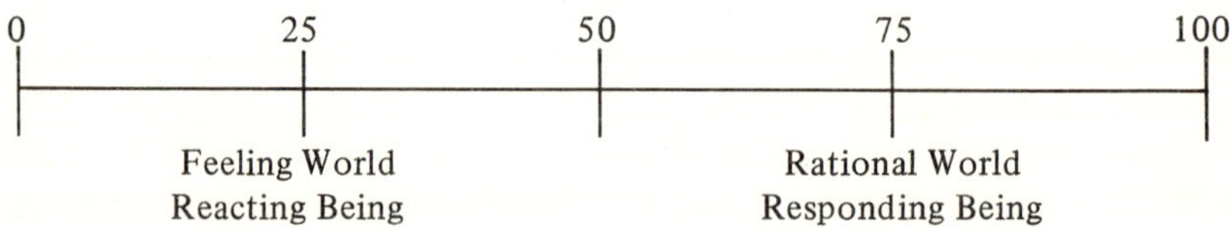

Structure 2

The scale is a continuum representing the range of human functioning from lowest level of differentiation to the highest level. The number 0 is the absolute low point and 100 is the highest point. At the zero point is the lowest level of self or the greatest degree of undifferentiation. At the other end of the scale is absolute individuality. These extreme ends of the continuum do not exist in reality. They are merely comparison points between which all individuals fall. The scale is not a measure of health, normalcy, or illness. It is a measure of each individual's tendency toward individuality or stuck togetherness. Bowen feels that higher level people are better equipped to handle crisis situations, but all can share equally in exhibiting dysfunctional behaviors. Lower scale people are more vulnerable to tension and exhibit higher rates of mental and physical illness. Higher scale people have a greater capacity for coping with stressful situations and a faster rate of recovery from tension related illness.

An individual's level of differentiation is seen in his interpersonal relationships and expressed in daily living. In order to understand an individual's behavior it is necessary to assess his level of functioning. To do this, Bowen has divided the scale into numerical categories and he has identified characteristics for each segment.

Low scale people are in the zero to twenty-five range. They live in a world dominated by affect. They have difficulty distinguishing between what feels good and what is good. Their lives are devoted to seeking relationships with others. Consequently, much of their daily behavior is focused on seeking love, attention, and approval from others. They are totally dependent on others for their selfhood. It is difficult to separate how they feel about themselves or events from how others feel about the same things. Minimal independent thought or decision making is observable. Decision, both minor and major, are made on the basis of what feels good now and on how other people evaluate the decisions. Dependency on others is thus fostered, and stuck togetherness is perpetuated. Low level individuals are more susceptible to dysfunction because they have little energy for independent problem solving. Most of their energy is devoted to pleasing themselves and others, so that in a crisis situation they are likely to collapse. If a crisis is not resolved, its continuance affects future coping and decision making. These people may be seen stumbling from one day to the next being continually buffeted by life's storms. No consistent life plan is evident, and short-term and long-term goals are absent. Low scale people may need periodic institutionalization in order to function even at a minimal level. Inpatient therapy would serve the function of protecting and recharging the inadequate self system. For these individuals, mental and physical illness is chronic since constructive change in their personhood is improbable.

People in the twenty-five to thirty segment of the scale possess most of the same qualities of those in the subtwenty-five range. They live in a world dominated by affective motivation and expend much of their energy seeking love and approval from others. Major life decisions are still based on feelings rather than rational exploration, and there is little energy left for goal directed behaviors. The major factor distinguishing this group from the lower is that there is a decrease in dependency and hence more differentiation of self.

The thirty to forty range is still characterized by the feeling orientation, but the people are less dominated by it. These people may be frequently referred to as being sensitive to others and as having the ability to observe subtle nuances in others' verbal and nonverbal behavior. The approval or disapproval of others is important in their own feeling states, but it is not crucial or always debilitating. The result is a more independent self system.

The rational part of the self system is gaining more control in people in the forty to fifty section of the scale. Feeling states are still dominant, but intellectual principles have a more tempering role in behavior and decision making. The intellect may now be used to strengthen interpersonal relationships. The individual who uses academic success for approval and acceptance is a prime example. Generally speaking, these people lack the strength of their own convictions and beliefs, but they are quick to know the thoughts and feelings of others. They may make good followers of authoritarian leaders, and they may be easily led into radical or self-righteous causes.

The upper half of the scale marks the swing to more rational dominance and a lowered affective orientation. Responding behaviors become more pronounced as opposed to the more reactive stance of the lower half. People in the fifty to sixty range of the scale respond more to rational principles, yet they are still controlled by the perceived demands of others. They know what they believe, yet they may hesitate to express their ideas for fear of offending others. As people advance to higher levels on the scale, they become more operationally clear about the differences between feelings and intellect. They are more comfortable expressing their own beliefs without becoming authoritarian, and they feel less need to defend their positions to outsiders. They have the ability to establish and initiate goal-directed behaviors, and they are also comfortable with intimate personal relationships. Independent and dependent characteristics of the self can be expressed appropriately, and differentiation of self is maximized.

Bowen believes that the scale is important for viewing personality in a theoretical perspective. It is valuable in estimating the overall potential of people and in making predictions about the general pattern of their lives. He emphasizes his belief that most people spend their lives at the same basic level they had as children. They tend to choose spouses who are at or near their basic level and produce children who also cluster around their level. An average distribution of children around the parental level would show some with higher levels of self and some with lower levels. It is those individuals with lower levels of differentiation who are more susceptible to physical and emotional illness in the future. Since they also tend to marry at their level and produce children higher and lower, the descending cycle is established. The decending levels of self create less differentiation in future generations and a higher incidence of dependent or psychotic behavior. Movement to higher levels of self is possible, but it requires considerable effort over a lifetime. The major focus of Bowen's therapy is to help individuals and families differentiate a few points higher on the scale.

Nuclear Family Emotional System

The concepts of triangling and differentiation of self are most clearly observed in Bowen's third concept of personality, the nuclear family emotional system. It is composed of the undifferentiated self system of father, mother, and children. A rough estimate of the spouses' level of differentiation conveys an idea about the quantity of undifferentiation potentially present for future trouble in the family. The greater the undifferentiation, the higher the potential for problems.

As two people develop a relationship and decide to marry, they form the basis of the new nuclear family. As previously mentioned, people seek spouses who have equivalent levels of self. They find these people to be most like them and believe that long term intimacy is more likely with more commonly shared attributes. The people involved, of course, are not aware of possessing a similar level of self. In the process of joining together, they develop a lifestyle that is compatible with their common levels of differentiation. From the outset, this lifestyle will determine the nature and kind of problems they will encounter in the future. The daily pressures of accommodating to one another and coping with outside forces creates pressure in the relationship. Problems develop from this intensity if the shared lifestyle is not differentiated enough to resolve these pressures. Some of the tension may be released through relationships with the extended family or through forces outside of the family network (work, friends, church, etc.). When the tension is too much for the system to handle in these ways, it will turn in on itself in an attempt to reestablish homeostasis. The emotional system of the family may focus the tension in one area or it may be distributed into several problem areas. If the intensity of emotion is so high that the family networks prove inadequate, problems may spill over into the community. Bowen identifies three problem areas that are most frequently used for tension reduction within the family network: marital conflict, dysfunction in one spouse, and/or impairment of one or more children.

Marital Conflict

The basic pattern in conflictual marriages is one in which neither spouse gives in to the other on major issues. These marriages are intense in terms of the amount of energy each invests in the other. The energy may be intellectual or emotional, positive or negative. The core of the problem is, however, that each is focused intensely on the self of the other. Commonly, the relationship cycles through intense closeness, conflict, the makeup, and another period of intense closeness. Marital conflict does not necessarily harm children unless the parents feel guilty and overcompensate in their reactions to them. Usually the parents are investing so much energy in their own relationship that they leave the children relatively uninvolved.

Dysfunction in One Spouse

Tension reduced in this area is achieved through the dynamics of dominance and submission. One partner becomes the active, dominant one, while the other is more passive and complacent. The passive one subjugates him/herself and becomes dependent on the direction of the dominant spouse, constantly adapting thinking, feeling, and behavior to meet the others needs. The spouse who is adaptive is the one who is most susceptible to dysfunction. The dysfunction can take many forms, such as drinking, gambling, antisocial behavior, physical illness, and lack of motivation. The dominant-submissive patterns can become enduring and highly resistive to change. For the partners involved, these behaviors provide an adequate, though dysfunctional, means of reducing tension and maintaining balance in their system.

Impairment of One or More Children

A commonly observed phenomenon, particularly by those professionals working with children, is the disturbed child. Bowen sees this problem as the third major way of reducing tension in the family. The disturbance between the parents is transmitted directly or indirectly to one or more of the children. The child becomes the focal point of the problem and removes the locus of intensity from the parental relationship. The child may eventually break down under the burden. Bowen considers this to be a primary dynamic of dysfunctional families and he devotes the fourth concept of the theory of personality completely to its elucidation.

Family Projection Process

The fourth concept deals with the basic process by which parental tensions are projected onto the children. It is present in the full range of problems from the mildest to the most severe. The most common pattern involves a mother who is overinvolved with her children and has minimal emotional involvement with her husband. The husband, however, is very sensitive to his wife's needs and supports her behavior to gain acceptance and approval. Hence, the projection is a result to parental immaturity, dependence, and undifferentiation. They are unable to function independently and reduce tension autonomously.

The mother is the key figure in the projection process. She has the most intense contact with her children and develops varying degrees of emotional attachment with each child. There is usually one child who might be a positive attachment, or it might be because the child was the most difficult to care for in infancy. This child may also be perceived as impaired from birth in comparison to the other children. Whatever the reason, this mother and child form a highly dependent, undifferentiated relationship. When tension is high in the mother, it is immediately transmitted to the child. It is as if there is an emotional umbilical cord between the two individuals. Tension is reduced in the mother when she projects her anxieties to the child. The father can unconsciously support this process since the result is favorable to the marital relationship. It may be the husband-wife relationship that is the source of the tension in the first place. By supporting the projection process, the father ensures a more comfortable relationship with his wife. They can both see the child as the problem in the family, rather than their own troubled marital relationship.

The father's support of his wife's projection is one alternative that he has. Another option is to withdraw from the mother-child relationship. This withdrawal can take any number of familiar forms. Abandonment of the family is an extreme example. The following are less extreme but equally effective forms of withdrawal: working long hours, work-related travel, drinking with the boys, and working alone in the basement. The list of avoidance behaviors is seemingly endless. However, the results are the same. The wife is allowed to project her anxieties onto a third party, the child; the source of the dysfunction, the marital relationship, is left relatively untouched. The father and mother avoid confronting their own troubled interactions, and the child becomes the disabled one.

It is interesting to note that the family projection process is quite selective in its choice of a victim. It was noted before that the chosen child is usually the one that is most attached to the mother. Typically, this child is also at the lowest level on the family differentiation scale. This low level child, because of the amount of undifferentiation and stuck togetherness, is most vulnerable to the projection process. He or she is the one who displays the least amount of independent functioning or autonomous reasoning. Bowen believes that certain categories of children are more vulnerable than others: oldest child, oldest boy or oldest girl (depending on which sex the mother favors), only boy or only girl, a child born when anxiety is high, and a child born with a defect. This process will continue throughout the lifespan of the family and will be perpetuated in future generations. When the chosen child is no longer available, the next lowest will be selected. When no children are available, other family members or nonfamily members will be brought into the triangle. The third side of the triangle must be filled in order to achieve balance in the system.

Multigenerational Transmission Process

This concept refers to the family projection process as it is viewed over several generations. In one generation, the parents project their undifferentiation to their lowest level child. As we have seen, this child is the most dependent and least capable of independent problem solving. When this child marries, he usually chooses a spouse who is at an equivalent level of undifferentiation. This new generation in turn projects their undifferentiation onto their children in varying degrees. The maximally involved child emerges with a lower level of self than the parents. The minimally involved child may emerge with about the same level of self. The more independent children may have higher levels of self.

As these children form their own families in the third generation, we can see movement up and down the self scale. Those who move up the scale may have a more productive life than their parents. Those who move down the scale encounter more difficulties and are less able to cope with life's stresses and strains. Over several generations, the low level, descending children may reach a point of undifferentiation where they are unable to deal with daily tension and conflict. They may be so impaired that they require frequent therapy or institutionalization. For Bowen, the multigenerational process provides a longitudinal view of a family's past, present, and future. It also provides information for the therapeutic process.

Emotional Cutoff

This is the most recent concept that Bowen has introduced into his theory of personality. It refers directly to the way that individuals deal with their dependency on the family when separation is imminent or has been accomplished. As we know, the greater the degree of undifferentiation, the lower an individual is on the self scale and the more dependent he is on his family. When this type of individual decides to begin separating from his family and to establish his own personhood or family, he encounters considerable conflict in himself and in other family members. The result is usually a state of pseudoindependence that generates anxiety and tension in his new relationship network. He will then repeat many of the same original family patterns in his new family. The multigenerational transmission process is in operation.

Bowen identifies several dysfunctional ways that individuals attempt emotional separation from their families. One way is to effect an emotional separation while still living in close physical proximity. The individual will attempt to isolate himself emotionally from the family by becoming increasingly uninvolved in family relationships. This emotional separation occurs in varying degrees of severity and can range from the typical adolescent rebelliousness to psychotic withdrawal. A second type of separation is seen in the individual who physically separates himself from the family by moving hundreds or thousands of miles away. The physical distance is an attempt to effect an emotional detachment. The third kind of separation is a combination of the first two, physical distance and emotional separation.

All three ways of separation are dysfunctional because the individual never differentiates himself from his parents. He is still stuck in the emotional system of the family, highly responsive to emotional stimuli, and unable to respond effectively in problem-solving situations. The dysfunction can manifest itself in several common ways such as physical illness, depression, impulsive behavior, and superficial relationships.

The higher level individual will not have to resort to these ineffective attempts at separation. Because he is more highly differentiated, he will encounter less conflict in separation. Since he is more independent, he will be better able to resolve the emotional attachments to his parents and to form new attachments in other relationships.

Sibling Positions

The seventh concept in the theory of personality deals with the rank of each child in the family. This rank is not necessarily concerned with birth order, but in many instances it is related to child chronology. The essence of the ranking is individual independence or levels of differentiation. The child with the lowest level of differentiation is labeled number one, the next lowest is number two, and so on. The child with the greatest display of independence is the last one in the ranking. In order to rank the children, Bowen relies on personality profiles that enumerate specific characteristics of low level, midlevel, and high level individuals. He believes these personality sketches are so accurate that he can evaluate past generations of the family and make predictions about future generations based on his observations of the present nuclear family.

Societal Regression

The final concept in the theory is also a relatively recent

addition. It was developed in order to more systematically apply family concepts to societal problems. Since both the family and society are systems, they operate using similar principles and can be evaluated with the same personality concepts.

Chronic anxiety is present in both families and societies. They both respond in a similar fashion depending on their levels of undifferentiation. The more undifferentiated a family or society is the more likely it is to seek short-term solutions to chronic, pervasive problems. The goal is to relieve the anxiety of the moment. These solutions tend to be emotionally based and depend considerably on the immediate affective climate. In this type of milieu, long range, thoughtful planning is at a premium. The family or society falls into a cycle of responding to each immediate crisis as it occurs, with no comprehensive plan for remediation or development. Historians and sociologists discuss the cyclical movement of societies and the rise and fall of various governments and cultures. Bowen, with the idea of societal regression, attempts to understand and explain the problems of a society. By applying his family systems concepts he sees the stress present in society as a triggering force in the undifferentiated ego mass. The less differentiated a society, the less likely it is to seek effective solutions and the more likely it is to develop dysfunctional symptoms. In successive generations, the society becomes increasingly more undifferentiated and consequently more emotionally unhealthy. Hence, society is regressing on the self scale, much like individuals and families. Eventually, the society crumbles when it is no longer able to cope with its problems. Bowen believes that the concept of societal regression is particularly critical today because of the seeming increase in world problems. If societies do not begin to differentiate to higher levels, human survival in the future is in jeopardy.

Key Words and Phrases

General systems theory
Stuck togetherness
Individuality
Low level
High level
Multigenerational transmission process

Undifferentiated	Differentiation
Family triangle	Emotional cutoff
Self scale	Sibling positions
Nuclear family emotional system	Societal regression

THERAPEUTIC PROCESS

The therapeutic process is based directly on the concepts of personality. Since the concept of the triangle is primary, the therapy focus is on the central triadic relationship. This central triangle is usually composed of the parents and one child. The involved child is probably the most undifferentiated sibling and is thus the object of the projection process. Through therapy, the central triangle (or any part of it) will be encouraged to change and differentiate to a higher level. If one part (or one triangle) changes, all other parts of the system must change according to system's principles. This change is particularly difficult to initiate and maintain since other elements in the system will be resisting any change. This situation is more noticeable when tension is high in the family. Anxiety triggers the projection process in the triangle. Any blockage in projection maintains tension, and the family fights to rid itself of that block so that it can reduce the tension. One of the first tasks of the therapist is to reduce the anxiety in the family and only later attempt to change the system. Premature movements for change may increase tension to the point where the family will reject therapy in the first few sessions.

Family therapy begins when the family first contacts the therapists. He tries to identify a specific reason for the contact and he may initially try to pinpoint specific short-term goals. All family members are requested to attend at least one family session. This gives the therapist first hand information about the workings of this system. As the therapy progresses, only the central family members may be asked to attend. Bowen believes that there is a point of diminishing returns if all members attend all of the time. Children become restless, and less involved members may be easily bored.

In the first step of the therapy process, the therapist attempts to establish a family orientation. He wants the family to begin viewing the problem as a total family problem and not just an aberration in one member. Frequently, the first therapeutic goal is to develop communication in the family. The therapist may ask many questions about the past and present functioning of the family and try to involve all members at one time or another. He is thus the catalyst and facilitator of communication in the family. Extensive communication may be new to a family, and they may need directive guidance to develop these behaviors. Family members may be pleased with the results of simply talking together. Everyone has a chance to express himself in a calm, less threatening environment. The establishment of a satisfying communication process in the first stage of therapy will predispose the family to greater change in the later phases of counseling.

The second step in the therapy process focuses directly on a detailed diagnosis of the family system. As the family communicates in the first few sessions, the therapist is observing the system in operation. He looks at the triadic networks and attempts to identify who belongs in the triangles and how the projection process works. He is assessing the level of individual and family undifferentiation, since this will give him a clue to the family's potential for change. The lower the level of undifferentiation the less likely the family is to make significant changes in their established patterns. Grandparents may be included in several sessions so that several generations may be seen interacting at one time. The entire observation stage is used to develop therapeutic goals for the family. The primary goal is to help the entire family differentiate to a higher level of self. However, specific goals need to be established to guide the therapist and the family in the months of therapy that lie ahead of them.

The third step in the therapy process is the most crucial and difficult phase. It is here that the first attempts at change will be made, and it is here that the family's resistance will be most strongly felt. A successful first step has developed freer communication in the family. The therapist, in the second stage, has assessed the family's process and levels of self. He is now ready to begin encouraging one family member to differentiate to a higher level of self. This family member is the one who has been identified as the most differentiated and most likely to respond to requests for change. As this member begins to act and express himself more independently, the family may attempt to block any movement toward individuality. Since increased independence is a threat to the system and increases tension, the family will try to inhibit the individual and draw him back into the family's emotional system. They may express anger and disappointment that one of their own would challenge or reject them. The differentiating one can be severely affected by these familiar messages. When he feels the family reaction, he may feel emotionally distressed or develop physical complaints. He may withdraw or run away. These attempts at emotional cutoff will be unsuccessful since true differentiation has not occurred. The individual will remain in turmoil, but the family system will be balanced. These balancing mechanisms in the system are emotional responses and caused by the lowered level of undifferentiation in the unit. Any attempts at change will be met by these emotional responses, and Bowen considers them to be a formidable barrier in every therapeutic process.

The therapist must attempt to counter these responses by encouraging the individual to respond in a nonemotional way. Rationality is the one effective countermove to emotionality. If the differentiating one can convince himself that he is doing the right thing, he may be able to resist the efforts of the family to draw him back into the ego mass. The therapist must be careful to avoid the family seeing him as working against their best interests. They must not see him supporting one member against the system. If the differentiating one can respond in a less emotional manner, he will break the old pattern and force the family into new realignments.

"I" statements are particularly useful at this point to aid the individual. By focusing on the individual's needs, expressed as "I" statements, the therapist can help the individual become more responsible for his own beliefs, feelings, and behaviors. Statements like, "I will...," "I can...," "I don't...," demonstrate to the family that this person is a separate self and must be dealt with as such. This new autonomy can create a chain reaction in the system and may develop new alternative responses in other members.

The therapist must remember that this is only the beginning of change in the system. An air of complacency with success or feelings of frustration at unsuccessful differentiation can allow the family the opportunity to revert back to their old balanced state. If the differentiating one continues to move in the direction of a higher level of self, the family may give one last intense effort to seduce him back into the mass. When the differentiating one successfully resists the most fervent efforts of the system to draw him back, the family accepts this new behavior and finds a new balanced state. Tension is reduced, and family members accept their new positions vis-à-vis one another.

This first successful attempt at differentiation is frequently followed by a period of tranquility in the system. Individuals can be allowed to savor this temporary state until another member chooses to develop more individuality and begins his differentiating process. As this phenomena generalizes to other family members, the family moves to a higher level of self. This is the fourth step in the therapy process. Eventually, all members may differentiate to higher levels with the continual direction and encouragement of the therapist. When significant, widespread change has occurred in the family, therapy may be terminated.

The most effective process of family therapy involves all family members at one time or another. Total family involvement is particularly effective during the first ten to fifteen sessions. When therapy goes beyond these limits, it is recommended that only the most involved members be required to participate. Intense therapy can then continue for several years until comfortable change is accomplished.

At times, it is not possible to involve all family members from the outset. Only one spouse may be receptive to counseling. Both parents may resist and only consent to the involvement of the disturbed child. In any case, Bowen would proceed with the therapy process feeling that change can still occur based on systems principles. Short-term symptom relief may be the most realistic prognosis, however, significant family change is possible depending on the level of differentiation of the individuals involved in therapy. Their differentiation may generalize to other family members through the process of daily living.

Key Words and Phrases

Undifferentiated individual	Movement to differentiate
Central family members	Emotional responses
Family therapy orientation	"I" statements
Family systems diagnosis	Generalization of differentiation

CHAPTER 3

STRUCTURAL MODEL

DESCRIPTION OF MAJOR THEORIST

SALVADOR MINUCHIN, M.D.

PROFESSIONAL POSITIONS. Director, Philadelphia Child Guidance Clinic. Professor, University of Pennsylvania, Pediatrics and Child Psychiatry. Psychiatrist-in-Chief, Childrens Hospital of Philadelphia.

MAJOR PUBLICATIONS. *Families and Family Therapy*. Cambridge, Mass., Harvard University Press, 1974. *Families of the Slums*. New York, Basic Books, 1967.

INTRODUCTION TO THEORY

STRUCTURAL Family Therapy is certainly not the first nor the most widely understood theory that emphasizes the influence of society on the development and growth of the individual. It is one of a long line of therapies that postulate the predominance of environmental factors as determinants of behavior. The individual influencing and in turn being influenced by his social mileau is a central theorem in most modern theories. Structural Family Therapy is no exception. Many current theories view the family as a microcosm of the social milieu, and the individual's primary interpreter of societal values, rules, and behaviors. The individual is socialized in the family unit. His adaption or maladaption to society is formed in this most basic unit. Functional and dysfunctional behaviors are taught and perpetuated by the family. Is it not logical then to work with the source of behavior if you are seeking to modify or change it? Family theorists, of course, answer, "yes!"

Minuchin, being no exception, has developed an elaborate therapy model for dealing with the most basic unit of society. However, unlike other theorists who focus exclusively on interpersonal interactions or family communication processes, he directs his energy toward the structure of the family. He believes that an individual's behavior can be significantly changed by altering the structure of the family system. Hence, the title of his theory is *Structural Family Therapy*. This emphasis on structural change permeates all aspects of the theory and technique, and it can be considered the primary differentiating factor from other theories. Structural theory does not ignore communication or reinforcement patterns in a family, but rather it incorporates these processes into an analysis of the structure and substructures of the unit. Treatment programs are then designed to restructure the family system and thereby change or modify individual members' behavior.

THEORY OF PERSONALITY

Minuchin conceives of the personality of a family as consisting of four major interdependent concepts. These concepts describe the life of the family as it deals with everday problems. They form the theoretical framework that the therapist will use to evaluate the functional and dysfunctional elements of each individual family. The concepts are considered to be universal. That is, they apply to families in general as well as to each individual family that a therapist will see. Based on an evaluation of the family using the four major concepts, the therapist will design a treatment plan to change various aspects of the structure of the family. Change in the structure will necessarily create change in individual members of the family.

It is important to stress the interdependent nature of the concepts. Their existence and functionality are dependent on one another. Each does not exist in isolation. However, for the purposes of this presentation, each concept will be discussed individually.

Family Structure

The idea of family structure is the first major concept of the theory. Minuchin sees the basic structure as consisting of sets of transaction between members of the family. These transactions have verbal and nonverbal components, and may be known or unknown to individuals in the family. Frequently, individual members are unaware of the majority of the transactions that exist in their family. Minuchin says that these transactions are actually complementary demands that are communicated between family members. The demands may be well-structured and follow definite patterns that are unique to that family. They are not random spurious events. When seen in totality, they form a tightly knit fabric that determines the essence of each individual family. They serve as the regulator of how a family will function in day-to-day and long-term situations.

According to Minuchin, transactions regulate behavior in two ways:

1. They represent a power hierarchy in the family. This hierarchy consists of various levels of authority and decision making.
2. They are the ways mutual expectations are determined and met. These expectations are negotiated over years of give and take.

The actual transaction and the events surrounding them may be buried in personal history and long since forgotten. However, the network that was established is present and subject to instant response.

The structure of a family has its origin when two individuals decide to form a relationship and perhaps marry. This couple forms the first set of transactions in order to handle the daily routine of living. This situation, which is actually a process that develops in the early stages of marriage, forms the basis for the family's lifelong development. The couple must learn to develop mutually satisfying ways of meeting each other's needs. Minuchin calls these means of satisfaction *spouse functions.* They are the ways in which a husband and wife interact between themselves and also with the outside world. The spouse functions are the core of the nuclear family. They may be seen as unique to that couple, however, the extended family may have considerable input into the development of this first set of transactions. Parents, brothers and sisters, aunts and uncles, and grandparents may be determining factors in how the new family develops its style of living.

The birth of the first child signals a radical change in the nuclear family structure. Each child introduces a new set of transactions. New demands must be incorporated into the structure, and new mutual commitments must be made between individuals. These new demands and commitments may represent a potent growth force in the nuclear and the extended family. Individuals may develop new ways of relating that are more satisfying and rewarding than the old ways. However, the birth of children may also germinate the seeds of dysfunction and destruction.

The primary task of the couple when the first child is born is to develop a new set of transactions. Minuchin labels these new transactions as *parent functions.* They are different from the spouse functions. A couple may have difficulty separating the two sets of functions. This separation difficulty is frequently the source of dysfunction in the family. Personal difficulties between the husband and wife may be enacted through parental functions. In other words, spouse disagreements may be acted out through the father and mother roles. Satisfactions not gained in the spouse relationship may be sought and achieved through and with the children.

Subsystems

The concept of subsystems within the family structure is the second postulate of the structural theory of personality. The structure that develops in a nuclear family or an extended family is too complex to meet the individual needs of each of its members. It is also impossible for all individuals in the family to attend to the specific aspects of maintenance of the structure all of the time. In other words, there must be a division of labor in the total system so that specific elements of the system will function effectively and efficiently. Subsystems are the divisions that families construct to carry out the essential functions of the system. A subsystem may consist of one individual in the family or several members at any one time. The composition of a subsystem may be rigidly defined or it may be relatively open and fluid. In well-functioning families, the membership in a subsystem is determined by the task at hand.

Individuals can move into and out of subsystems without major changes in the total system. Dysfunctional families, on the other hand, frequently present rigid subsystem patterns or unfocused distorted subsystem arrangements.

Subsystems are the primary mechanism that a family uses to differentiate its functions and to carry them out. (Their composition may be determined by generational associations, by sexual identity, by topics of interest, or by specific designated functions.) Each individual in the family may belong to several different subsystems at one time. In this context, the subsystem may be conceived of as the primary socializing agent in our society. Individuals must learn to communicate, negotiate, and cooperate with one another in order to accomplish the functions of the subunit. The subsystem can be an excellent training ground for individuals to develop their own personhood and their group identity.

The first subsystem that forms in a family is the spouse subsystem. The marital pair comprise the sole constituents of this grouping. Membership in this unit is not open to any other members of the system. There are specific functions that this subsystem must perform and these can only be accomplished by the husband and wife. Traditional marital transactions are the way that functions are fulfilled in this subunit.

The second subsystem that is typically formed in the family is the parental subsystem. The parental figures fulfill the primary authority and nurturing aspects of the unit. Father and mother typically reside in this subsystem. However, other family members may assume parental roles in the absence of the traditional authority figures. A parental subsystem can include a mother and an older son or daughter, a maternal grandmother and a father, or several other more typical combinations. The composition of the subsystem is probably not as important as the role assignments and responsibilities that its members accept. Well-functioning families usually have clearly defined and articulated role designations and responsibilities.

The third category of subunits is the sibling subsystem. There may be a number of sibling subsystems in one family depending on the size of the family, and specific nature of its functions. An only child would comprise the sibling subsystem in his family. When several children are present, they typically form shifting subsystems, each organized around a common focus, i.e. gender, interest, etc.. Sibling subsystems are as important to the health and development of the family as are the parental and spouse units. Each has a critical role to play in the developmental process. Structure 3 illustrates how subsystems may be depicted.

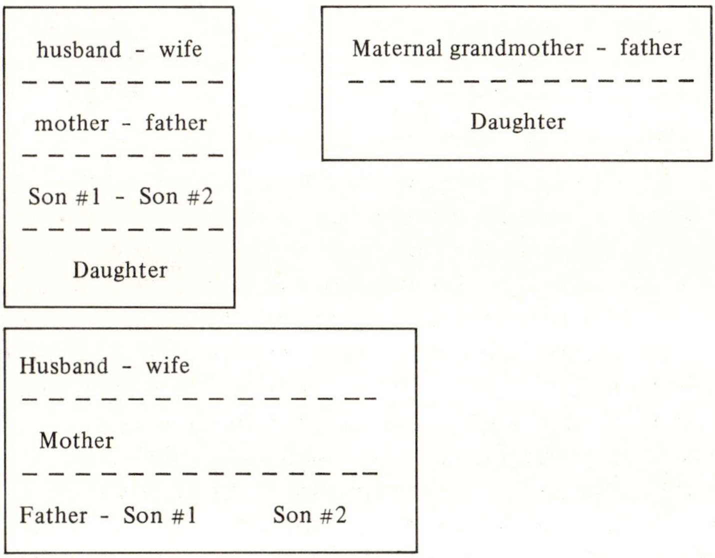

Structure 3

Subsystem Boundaries

The third major concept is that of subsystem boundaries. They are the rules of the subsystem that define who participates in it and how they participate. Efficient family functioning dictates that these rules be clearly defined and communicated to all family members so that the functions of that subsystem can be accomplished. There should be clearly drawn lines of responsibility and authority. Yet the boundaries must be flexible enough to allow input from members in other subsystems. The clarity and nature of the boundaries may be more important than the actual composition of the subsystem. An older son or daughter may perform effectively in the parental subsystem, provided the boundaries are appropriately established.

Minuchin identifies three types of boundaries that families establish to differentiate subsystems. These three are actually a continuum from very rigid to very diffuse (see Structure 4).

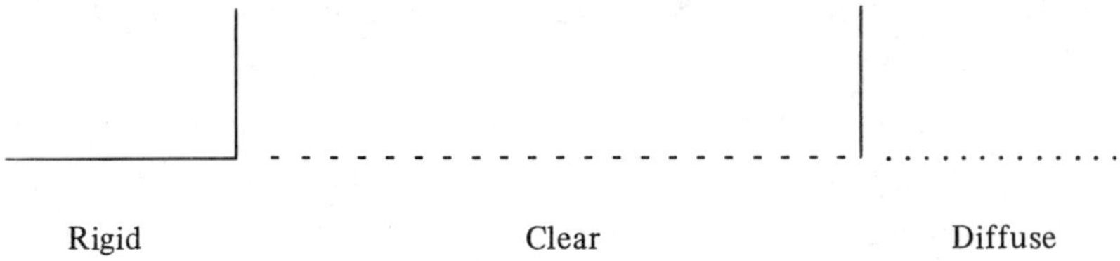

Structure 4

Minuchin depicts a rigid boundary as a straight unbroken line. Rigid boundaries allow minimal interaction between subsystems. Communication becomes difficult, if not impossible, in a family with rigid boundaries. Individuals may be isolated and forced to function autonomously. There is little opportunity for mutual support, shared experiences, or aspects of interdependence in daily living. Individuals may respond to one another only when faced with traumatic experiences. The results of rigid boundaries are disengaged subsystems.

At the other end of the continuum is the family with diffuse or blurred subsystem boundaries. Minuchin depicts this type of boundary with a dotted line. A family with diffuse boundaries is characterized by overinvolved, overdependent interactions. The membership and functions of subsystems is so poorly defined that members cannot differentiate who does what, when, or how it is to be accomplished. Responsibility for subsystem functions is dispensed randomly among and between family members. There are few clearly drawn lines of authority or responsibility. Tension or conflict that affects one member is dispersed and eventually affects all of the members. (Individual responsibility is discouraged.) This may lead to an ineffective lack of tension reduction and/or lack of problem resolution. At best, random and confused problem solving is the result.

Rigid and diffuse boundaries are extremes on the continuum and may exist primarily in highly disorganized or dysfunctional families. However, aspects of each are probably present in all families from time to time. Clear boundaries are more commonly found in functioning families that possess at least a minimum of problem-solving ability. Minuchin depicts a clear boundary as a line of dashes. Clear boundaries are characterized by open communication, protectiveness, and freedom. They provide protection for subsystem members so that they can fulfill subsystem functions. They provide privacy and security for individual members. The mother can feel that her authority and decision making will not be undermined by a demanding child. Mother and daughter can work together effectively without undue interference, e.g. jealousy, from father. At the same time, clear boundaries provide access to a subsystem from another subsystem or individual. Children can feel free to have a voice in family matters and share in decision making. Arbitrary, unsatisfying actions or decisions are minimized. Clear boundaries can provide the opportunity for the development of satisfying levels of individuality and mutuality in all family members.

In Structure 5 the family structure as a whole is differentiated from the outside world by clear boundaries that allow input from without and provide satisfying contact for individual family members with the environment. At the same time, family functioning is protected from undue outside influence. Family subsystems are characterized by the same qualities.

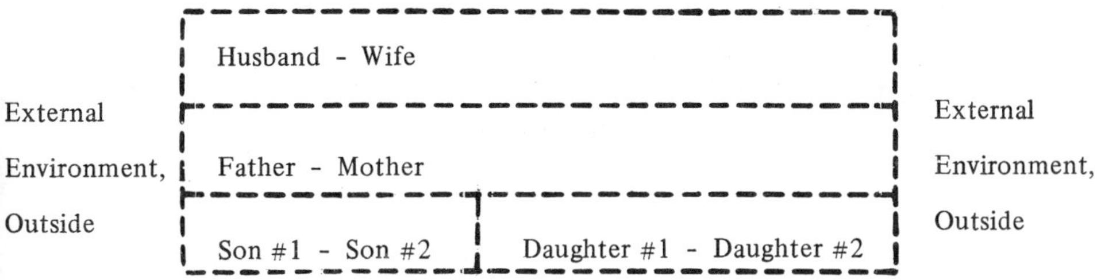

Structure 5

Adaption to Stress

Stress in daily living is inevitable, perhaps even necessary for growth and change to occur. This is true for the individual, but also relevant to the family constellation. The family is subject to internal stress emanating from developmental changes in its own members and its own subsystems. There are also external pressures affecting the family. These outer pressures may be directed at individual members, or they may affect the total structure as it attempts to relate and cope with the world at large. Individuals and families respond to these internal and external pressures in a variety of ways — some functional and some dysfunctional.

The fourth concept in the Structural Theory of personality deals with the sources of stress effecting a family, and how families adapt to tension situations. Minuchin identifies four sources of stress that affect families directly, and gives examples for each:

1. *Stressful Contact of One Member with Extrafamilial Forces* — The father may be experiencing difficulty at work and cannot express his tension directly to his boss. Hence, he will come home and criticize his wife for not keeping the house clean. The wife in turn will instead badger the children for not spending enough time on their homework. The stress that was initially contained in one member has been projected onto others, and reverberates through the entire structure. Each family member may have his or her own unique source of stress from outside forces. If these are not handled appropriately, they can all create dysfunction in the family.
2. *Stressful Contact of the Whole Family with Extrafamilial Forces* — This type of situation produces an immediate impact on all or most family members. Common situations would include the following:
   a. A job transfer to a new and perhaps different community.
   b. A farm family moving to an urban environment in search of greater employment opportunities.
   c. A family entering the United States from a foreign country.
   d. An economic recession or strike affecting the family financial resources.
3. *Stress at Transitional Points in the Family* — There are a number of common events that may occur with relative frequence in a family that can be considered critical transi-

tional points. The following are several of the more common ones:

a. The birth of the first child.
b. Children entering school for the first time. Perhaps the first and the last child create the most turmoil.
c. Parents' birthdays that are perceived as being critical, e.g. thirtieth, fortieth, fiftieth, for one reason or another.
d. Children entering adolescence.
e. Mother returning to the work force.
f. Children leaving home for school, for work, or to establish their own independence.

4. *Stress Around Idiosyncratic Problems.* Examples of these would include the presence of a chronically ill member or a retarded child.

The first two sources of stress are directly related to sources outside of the family structure that may have a profound effect on the internal workings of the unit. The final two are internal problems that may affect one or all of the family members. Whether the effect is minimal or catastrophic is dependent on how the family manages the stress and adapts its structure to that pressure.

Every family attempts to adapt to the stress in ways that will preserve the integrity of the structure. Minuchin believes that it is inconceivable that a family would deliberately attempt to destroy itself. The dysfunctional family may present strong evidence of self-destructiveness, but this is not conscious or purposeful. Self-destructive behaviors are seen as distorted ways of actually preserving the family structure. For example, the pathological family may shut out all outside input in order to save itself. Therapists regularly encounter profound resistance to change in dysfunctional families. (The wagons are drawn into a tight circle and the gates of the fort are tightly closed, so to speak.) The unhealthy family may also increase its rigidity in the face of stress. Instead of seeking and accepting new alternatives for dealing with problems, they will resort to the old inappropriate solutions or transactional patterns. Creativity, independence, and growth are stifled. The healthy family, on the other hand, will use the presence of stress for growth and expansion. Less rigidity and greater acceptance of outside input are good milestones for measuring the movement from pathology to health in family structures, subsystems, and individual members.

Key Words and Phrases

Family structure
Spouse functions
Parent functions
Subsystem
Sibling subsystem
Spouse subsystem
Parental subsystem
Boundaries
Rigid boundaries
Diffuse boundaries
Clear boundaries
Disengaged family
Enmeshed family

THERAPEUTIC PROCESS

A family usually enters therapy because of their concern about an individual member. The presenting problem(s) may cluster around this individual, and he is seen by the family as unusual, deviant, or troubled. Family therapists routinely label this individual as the identified patient. However, Minuchin and other family therapists do not consider the individual's symptoms in isolation, but rather as system-maintaining devices. The symptoms may in fact be an expression of a family dysfunction, or at the very least be supported by the system. In either case, according to Minuchin, the symptoms are being reinforced by the system. Restructuring of the family is necessary.

Steps in Process

In order to treat a dysfunctioning family, Minuchin has developed an elaborate and well-structured therapeutic process. It can be considered the most comprehensive expression of a counseling process in the field of family therapy to date. His process consists of three major steps:

1. He joins the family in a position of leadership.
2. He unearths and evaluates the underlying family

structure.

3. He creates circumstances that will allow the transformation of the family structure.

Therapeutic Maneuvers

Minuchin uses two basic therapist maneuvers to actualize this process with the family. Each one contains specific strategies that are used on a moment-to-moment basis in the session.

Joining/Accommodating

Joining operations are methods used when the therapist is attempting to relate directly to family members or the family system. Empathy and support are key counselor behaviors at this point. Accommodating operations are used when the therapist is adjusting himself to achieve joining. In order to join a family system, the therapist must adopt the family's style and blend into it. He must experience the life of the family from within, but still maintain his own professional integrity and objectivity so as to observe the workings of the family. Minuchin identifies a number of accommodation techniques that he uses successfully:

MAINTENANCE. An accommodation technique for providing planned support of individuals, subsystems, and alliances. Supporting specific behaviors or verbalizations may increase their strength and independence.

TRACKING. The therapist follows the family's communications through the ebb and flow of a session. The counseling techniques of clarification, amplication, and approval are used at this time. These behaviors help to reinforce and confirm individuals and subsystems.

MIMESIS. The therapist attempts to adopt the family's style of relating and conform to its affective range. If the family is slow speaking and nonexpressive, then the therapist behaves in a similar manner. If expletives are used frequently, the therapist will adopt this mode of speaking.

Minuchin considers all accommodation techniques to be restructuring techniques also. The first set of therapeutic maneuvers blends naturally and smoothly into the second type.

Restructuring

The second set of maneuvers are called restructuring techniques. They are used to confront and challenge the family in an attempt to produce movement or change. They are attempts by the therapist to intervene in the system and create movement toward therapeutic goals. They must unbalance the family system, and force the family to seek new alternatives and solutions. Minuchin identifies seven major restructuring techniques:

ACTUALIZING FAMILY TRANSACTIONAL PATTERNS. The therapist will stimulate interaction between family members so that he can observe their typical patterns. Nonverbal behavior is as important as verbal transactions. Occasionally individual's gestures, posture, or facial expressions contradict what they are actually saying. This technique is accomplished by using different tasks. The therapist may ask individuals to engage in a conversation rather than describe the events to him. He may force the family to talk to one another by refusing to answer or participate. Or he may ask members to change places and thus manipulate space in the family configuration.

MARKING BOUNDARIES. The boundaries that exist in a family between individuals or subsystems may be too rigid or too weak. With an enmeshed family, where the boundaries are too weak, he will try to strengthen them. With a disengaged family, the therapist will attempt to decrease the rigidity of boundaries. Marking boundaries is accomplished in several ways. The therapist may at first begin to delineate boundaries by helping the family to set new rules or negotiate old rules for each individual. This promotes autonomy and individuality. Secondly, he may try to strengthen subsystem boundaries by establishing specific functions for each subunit. For instance, parents or children may be asked to perform certain functions by and with themselves.

ESCALATING STRESS. Frequently, families in distress have developed inappropriate ways of decreasing the stress in their unit. Minuchin believes that it can be beneficial to heighten tension in a family in order to force them to accept restructuring. In order to do this he recommends that the therapist actively block dysfunctional transactional patterns when they occur, that he emphasizes differences between members, encourage conflict when it erupts and actively join alliances or coalitions against other family members. All of these behaviors are an attempt to force a healthier resolution of the stress that is present.

ASSIGNING TASKS. Specific tasks can be assigned to individuals or subsystems that are to be accomplished in the session or at home.

UTILIZING SYMPTOMS. The therapist must be cautious and skillful in his method of treating specific symptoms. Minuchin recommends a number of different and opposing ways that this problem might be handled. The therapist may wish to focus directly on the symptom and marshall the family's forces to help one individual. This is particularly useful in the case of overt neurotic symptoms like phobias. With another family, the therapist will exaggerate the symptom and increase its intensity hoping thereby to force the family to concentrate their energy on removing it. In other instances, with different symptoms or families, the therapist will deemphasize the symptom, move on to a new symptom, or relabel the symptom by calling it something else. The latter three methods are attempts to remove the reinforcement that an individual is receiving for having this symptom. It is an attempt to remove the secondary gain that may be inherent in symptomotology.

MANIPULATE MOOD IN FAMILY. When the therapist joins a family, he tries to adopt its level of affect. This helps him to be more attuned to the inner life of the family, but it can also promote restructuring. Minuchin cites examples of how a therapist can give an exaggerated imitation of a mood in order to counter the families reliance on that mode of interacting. For instance, if a mother is yelling at her child, the therapist will yell louder.

SUPPORT, EDUCATION AND GUIDANCE. The therapist assumes the role of a teacher by instructing the family to behave differently. That is, the parents may be told to give more individual attention to each of their children, or they may be told to spend more time together.

Joining/accommodating operations are related to the first step in the counseling process. At that point, the counselor is primarily interested in being accepted by the family as a helping agent and establishing an effective therapeutic relationship. Before restructuring or change can occur, he must evaluate the present state of the family and decide how he will intervene in the system. This process of evaluation comprises the second step in counseling. The therapist begins to diagnose the family structure based on the concepts of his theory of personality. He wants to develop working hypotheses from his observations and then design interventions to accomplish his therapeutic goals. Minuchin calls his process of evaluation an interactional diagnosis or structural diagnosis. This diagnosis focuses initially on the family's interactions. The therapist observes them together and participates whenever possible. He is looking for data in six major areas.

1. First he considers the family structure as a whole. What are its preferred transactional patterns, and what alternative patterns are available to it?
2. He evaluates the system's flexibility as well as its capacity for elaboration and restructuring.
3. He observes how sensitive individual members are to one another. Is this an enmeshed or a disengaged family?
4. He reviews the family life context, paying particular attention to sources of stress in or on the family, and methods of support available to the family.
5. He examines the family's current developmental stage and its performance of specific tasks that are appropriate for that stage.
6. He explores the ways in which an individual's symptoms are used or reinforced in the family structure.

Mapping

The information that is gathered is expressed in the form of a therapeutic map. The map will generate working hypotheses for the therapist, identify restructuring techniques that may be helpful, and establish short-term and long-term counseling goals. The map also serves as an ongoing evaluation of the therapeutic process. In actual practice, the therapist may construct a number of maps in one session or over the entire therapeutic process. They may be graphed on paper for the therapist's use, or they may be shared with the family at appropriate intervals. However, it may exist only in the mind of the therapist and provide a useful guide for him in planning present and future interventions.

Since mapping is unique to Structural Family Therapy, Minuchin has described the graphic process in detail. Structure 6 show the symbols that a therapist would use in constructing a map.

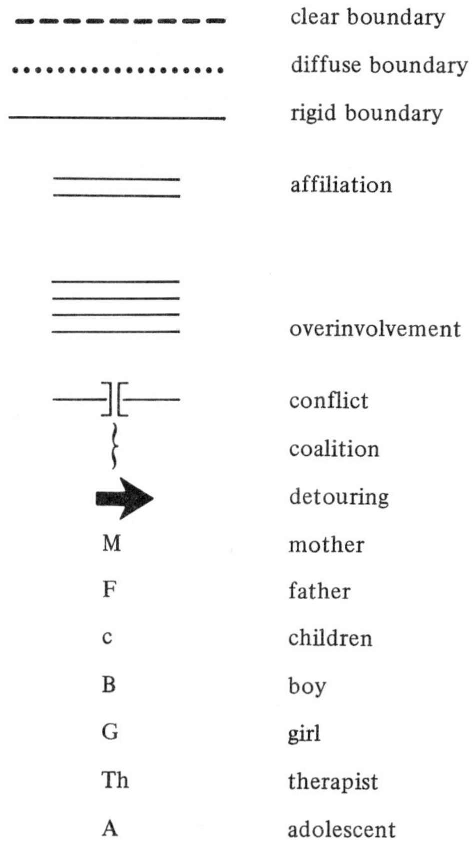

Structure 6

Structure 7 shows sample maps depicting various family

Spouse subsystem with clear boundary

Parental subsystem with clear boundary

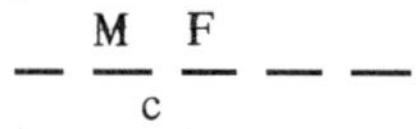

Sibling subsystem with clear boundary

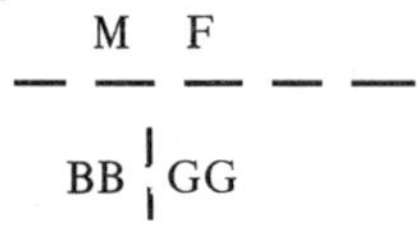

Coalition with diffuse boundaries

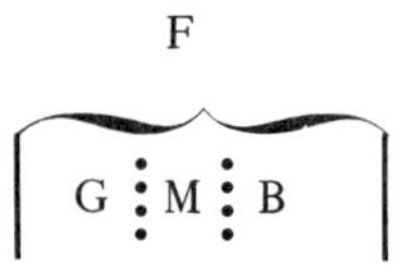

Conflict with rigid boundary

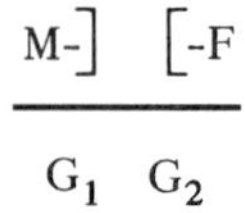

Affiliation with rigid and clear boundaries

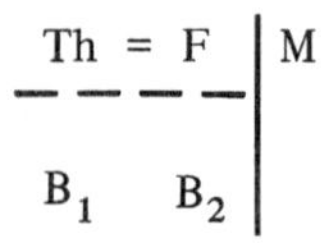

Overinvolvement with coalitions

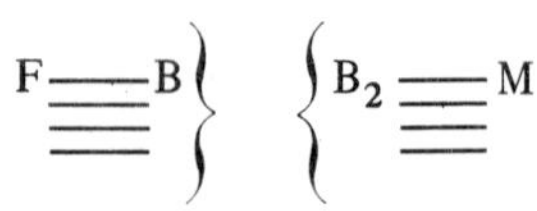

Detouring with clear and diffuse boundaries.

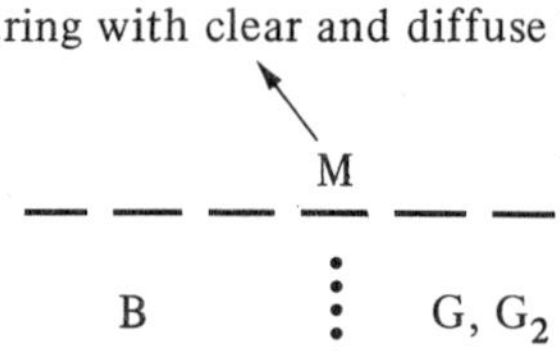

Structure 7

structures and subsystems.

The therapist will begin restructuring the family after he feels comfortable joining/accommodating the family and after he has gathered some interactional data. Restructuring is the third step in the counseling process and may begin early in the first session. More typically though, the therapist will wait till the latter part of the first session or till the second session to begin restructing in earnest.

The therapeutic process is terminated when both the family and the therapist feel that a structure now exists in the family for dealing with future stress situations in appropriate ways. The therapist is satisfied that his therapeutic goals for restructuring have been satisfied. The family is pleased that it can resolve present difficulties and that it has a process for dealing with future problems.

Key Words and Phrases

Joining
Accommodation
Restructuring
Maintenance
Tracking
Mimesis
Actualizing Transactional Patterns
Marking boundaries
Escalating stress

Symptom focus
Symptom exaggeration
Relabel symptom
Mood manipulation
Structural diagnosis
Family map
Affiliation

Coalition
Detouring

CHAPTER 4

SOCIAL LEARNING MODEL

DESCRIPTION OF MAJOR THEORIST

GERALD R. PATTERSON, Ph.D.

PROFESSIONAL POSITIONS. Professor, University of Oregon. Director, Oregon Research Institute.

MAJOR PUBLICATIONS. *Families.* Champaign, Illinois, Research Press, 1975. *Living with Children.* Champaign, Illinois, Research Press, 1968.

INTRODUCTION TO THEORY

THE Social Learning Approach is the result of the work of Doctor Gerald Patterson at the Oregon Research Institute in Eugene, Oregon. For more than ten years, he and his staff have been treating children with behavior problems. In addition to the treatment aspects of the program, Patterson has been conducting research on the efficacy of his treatment procedures. At the institute, children are not treated in isolation. The entire family is the focus of treatment. The child may be the initial focus of the referral, but the therapist views the problem as an outgrowth of faulty learning in the family. So in this sense, this approach is a family therapy model.

The Social Learning Approach is firmly grounded on the general principles of behaviorism. The operant learning concepts of B. F. Skinner form the core of the theory of personality. Since reinforcement is the key concept in operant conditioning, it is also the major variable in Patterson's theory. The therapeutic process relies heavily on the classic behavior modification techniques that have been widely disseminated and used in the past quarter century. In short, the Social Learning Approach is an adaption of behaviorism and behavior modification to the family unit. It is an application of tried and true learning principles to problems in families.

In the past, behaviorism has concerned itself primarily with individual animal and human behavior. (General and specific learning principles have been developed that have revolutionized the educational process on an international scale.) Much research and practice has been devoted to isolating and changing specific individual behaviors. Behaviorism has become a major theory in the field of individual psychotherapy. Learning principles have also been widely applied to groups. Today, classroom teachers commonly use reinforcement techniques to control and change the behavior of their students. Business and industry use aspects of learning theory to increase its employees motivation and productivity. All aspects of society have been touched by the behavioristic theory. It is only natural, then, that learning theory should be applied to families and that there should be a behavioristic family therapy model. The Social Learning Approach is this type of model.

Most of a person's early learning occurs in the family. Family members are an individual's first exposure to basic living skills and behaviors. Parents are teaching their children certain behaviors from their first moment of contact. As the infant is introduced into the home, older brothers and sisters, grandparents, and any other people who have significant contact with the child are teaching him. He, in turn, is also teaching them how to behave with him and in his presence. It is a mutual learning process; all family members train one another. Some of the basic behaviors that are taught are skills for living with other people in society. Hence, the title for this model is the *Social Learning Approach.*

Essentially, people learn what they are taught, but they are not always as discriminating as they should be. In some cases, people do not have control over what they learn. They respond automatically to certain reinforcements in their environment. In this and other ways, positive and negative behaviors are learned and incorporated into the personality. Parents do not always know what they are teaching their children. They may feel that they are emphasizing a positive behavior, when in fact they are reinforcing a negative action. This is frequently the case with poor child management techniques and acting out behaviors of younger children. Examples of these could be a child's temper tantrum or a child talking back to his parents.

The more family members know about what they are teaching each other the more control they can have over the content. Accidental learning is less likely to take place and positive learning is more apt to occur when people are aware of what they are doing. Through awareness and the consistent application of learning principles, a family can change the immediate social environment in which they live. The remainder of this chapter is devoted to a presentation of Doctor Patterson's ideas about how to initiate and maintain family change. The first part of the last two sections will discuss general aspects of behaviorism and behavior modification. The latter portion of each deals specifically with Patterson's application of these general ideas to family therapy.

THEORY OF PERSONALITY

General Behavioristic Theory

The Social Learning Approach is primarily based on the operant conditioning model developed by B. F. Skinner. This theory emphasizes the overwhelming influence of environmental factors as determiners of an individual's behavior. Hereditary factors play only a small part in what happens to a person from birth to death. According to this theory, all behaviors are learned reactions to the environment. All of our present day behaviors are a result of past conditioning in our environment. Since parents and family are a significant part of a child's environment, his present day behaviors are determined by the past reactions of his family. A person carries into adulthood many of the conditioned experiences of his early years.

In the Behavioristic theory, personality is a set of learned or acquired behaviors. These behaviors are lawful. They follow predictable patterns, and they occur in a similar manner time after time. By knowing the pattern of a given behavior and the factors in the immediate environment, we can anticipate and predict specific actions. With this prior knowledge, we can design strategies to change or alter behavior in the future.

In the course of our daily living, we have learned to react to general and specific stimulus situations in prescribed ways. These responses are part of fixed patterns that can be observed and altered. By altering the response patterns, we can change specific unwanted behaviors. The following is a major premise of behaviorism: what was learned, can be unlearned. In other words, we can replace present, dysfunctional behaviors with new, more appropriate actions. Since the environment (or aspects of the environment) is the major learning and reinforcing agent, manipulating or changing the environment will change behavior.

Reinforcement is the key factor in this change process. A major tenet of behaviorism states that reinforcement increases the likelihood of a response occurring again. Conversely, nonreinforcement decreases the likelihood of a response reoccurring. Behaviorists call the latter process extinction. Simply stated, if we want a person to behave in a certain manner we must reinforce that behavior. If we wish to extinguish a present action, we must not reinforce or negatively reinforce that response. Depending upon the situation, a behaviorist may want to increase or decrease certain behaviors. In order to do this, it is helpful to identify different kinds of reinforcement and various levels of reinforcement. Essentially, there are four kinds of reinforcement.

POSITIVE REINFORCEMENT. This category contains any reinforcer that motivates an individual to repeat his behavior in order to gain a reward. The determination of what is positive for a person is an individual decision. What is desirable to one person is neutral or repugnant to another. For instance, we may believe that all children like candy and that they would be positively motivated by an offer to receive a candy bar. However, there are children who dislike certain kinds of candy and would not perform to receive this type of reward. In this case, the reward would not be positive and would not cause the behavior to reoccur. For them, candy is not a positive reinforcer. Incorrectly identifying reinforcers can lead to the failure of a behavioral program. In short, it is critical for the therapist to identify positive reinforcers on an individual basis.

NEGATIVE REINFORCEMENT. This second kind refers to the removal of an aversive stimuli. The response that follows it is strengthened because something unwanted is removed or withdrawn. The person is negatively reinforced because the aversive stimulus is taken away and he feels more comfortable. For example, a father may ask his son to perform a certain task at home. The child then refuses and proceeds to throw a temper tantrum. Consequently, the father removes his original request. The father has just negatively reinforced the tantrum behavior. The child will be likely to repeat that behavior because the aversive stimulus (the request to perform a task) was withdrawn.

PUNISHMENT. It can be defined as the presentation of any unpleasant, unwanted, or aversive stimuli into an individual's environment. The presence of the aversive stimuli reduces the strength of the behavior that is presently occurring. Many behaviorists advise against the use of punishment because it can generalize to other desirable behaviors and thus reduce their strength also. There is also a concern about the modeling effect of punishment on the receiver. A person, particularly a child, may choose to imitate the aggressive behavior of the punisher in future life situations. Common examples are physical punishment, electric shocks, and harsh world of approbation.

NON-REINFORCEMENT. This final category refers to the removal of any reinforcement for a given behavior. It may take one of two forms: the planned absence of any reinforcement for an individual behavior or the removal of the subject from the reinforcing situation. In the first instance, the individual is ignored when he behaves in an inappropriate way. The classroom teacher pointedly ignores the attention-getting behavior of a student. Or, a mother ignores the young child who is throwing a temper tantrum. In the second instance, the subject is physically removed from the reinforcement situation and placed in a neutral, nonreinforcing environment. The most common example of this technique is time-out. It is widely used in school, institutional, and family environments.

In addition to the four kinds of reinforcement, we can identify three different levels of positive and negative reinforcement. They are listed in hierarchical order from one to three. Number one, material reinforcement, is considered to be the lowest level because it appeals to the basic level of animal and human nature. It is also the most difficult to maintain for long periods of time. The highest level is number three, intrinsic reinforcement. It is considered the highest level because it appeals to man's higher nature, namely, personal satisfaction and internal pleasure.

MATERIAL REINFORCEMENT. This basic level involves the presentation of material objects after a behavior has occurred. Again, the person must perceive the object as desirable in order for it to be a positive motivator. He must also be aware that if he repeats the behavior, he will receive another desired object. Hence, the person repeats the behavior to gain the sought after reward. Common examples of material reinforcers are paychecks, tokens, candy, and prizes in a raffle.

NON-MATERIAL OR SOCIAL REINFORCERS. This is the next highest level of reinforcement. It involves the presentation of any nonmaterial reinforcers. Common examples include praise, physical attention, and verbal admonitions. It is considered to be a higher level of reinforcement because it appeals to the more human and emotional aspects of the person.

INTRINSIC REINFORCEMENT. This third level does not involve the action of a second person as a reinforcer. Essentially, the individual acts as his own reinforcer for a given behavior. The performance of that behavior creates enough pleasure and satisfaction internally that the individual chooses to repeat it to gain further internal satisfaction. This is considered to be the highest level of reinforcement, because the individual is behaving in ways that please himself and not only others. An example of internal reinforcement is the master craftsman or artist who takes great pains to build an object as perfectly as possible. He could take less effort and time and receive the same monetary and social rewards. However, he strives for perfection in order to gain the personal satisfaction that only his best work will give him.

Generally speaking, the behaviorist prefers to use material reinforcers only in the beginning of a modification or learning process. The goal is to move to the higher levels as soon as possible. This usually happens when the new behavior is occurring at an acceptably high rate, or when a behavior is at the point of extinction. The more mature the subject, the quicker and easier it is to move to the second and third levels.

The following summarize the major points of this brief presentation:

Personality is a set of learned behaviors.
These behaviors are learned in the environment.
They are lawful and predictable.
Past conditioning is an important determiner of present behavior.
Specific behaviors can be unlearned.
New behaviors can be conditioned to take their place.
Reinforcement is the primary tool that is used.

Social Learning Approach

Patterson accepts and uses most of the concepts of operant conditioning that have just been presented. The major deviation is that the focus of intervention is not an individual family member but rather the entire family interaction pattern. He believes that family members teach one another how to behave. This is particularly so in the case of social behaviors. They are not always aware of what they are teaching or how they are reinforcing specific behaviors. This unawareness is one of the major problems in dysfunctional families. Providing awareness and insight is a primary focus of therapy.

Reinforcement is the key concept and technique in the Social Learning Approach. People, particularly parents, can be taught when and how to give reinforcement. In fact, all family members can train themselves and each other to be reinforcers. Individuals in the family acting as role models are an important source of learning. Patterson suggests the use of both positive and negative reinforcers used in conjunction with one another whenever possible. He advocates the use of social reinforcement, particularly that which shows full attention toward the subject. Simply saying thank you, touching, hugging, and kissing are all nonmaterial reinforcers. On the other hand, behaviors can be decreased by using nonreinforcement techniques or punishment. Whatever the choice is for a particular behavior, it must be consistently applied over long periods of time to affect change. The main emphasis in this approach is to strengthen some behaviors and weaken others. Family members can do this by positively reinforcing those behaviors that they want to increase and not reinforcing those that they want to decrease or extinguish. (Reinforcement is gradually decreased once a behavior is occurring at an acceptable rate.) In order to do this, in most families, it requires an organized plan consisting of specific goals and change techniques.

Patterson prefers to use positive reinforcement and nonreinforcement whenever possible. He believes that negative reinforcement and punishment are counterproductive and sometimes destructive in the learning process. He refers to hitting, yelling, and harsh scolding as the most inappropriate ways of handling children. By using these type of punishments, parents may actually be training their children to punish themselves and others. His position seems to be underscored by the most recent studies on child aduse. It appears that a large portion of parents who abuse their children were abused when they were young. They were trained, in other words, to be punishers and abusers. Patterson also makes the point that parents can be reinforced for being punishers because it frequently works in decreasing behavior for the immediate moment. However, it is usually ineffective for any prolonged period of time or as a technique for permanent behavior change. In a sense, when parents use punishment effectively their children are training them to behave in dysfunctional ways. The children are reinforcing their parents, by temporarily decreasing an unwanted behavior, to behave in inappropriate ways as punishers.

Some types of punishment may be appropriate in certain situations. The use of mildly aversive natural consequences or the use of time-out procedures could be used effectively to decrease problem behaviors. However, whenever an individual uses mildly aversive techniques, they should be paired with positive reinforcement of a competing behavior. If punishment is used by a family member, Patterson suggests several guidelines. First of all, the behavior modifier should intervene early in the problem situation. Do not wait until the behavior is out of control. Use time-out procedures or mildly aversive techniques everytime the behavior occurs. Always remain calm and do not get emotionally involved in the problem. And finally, positively reinforce any competing behavior. By following these suggestions, parents and other family members can avoid the negative effects of using punishment.

In summary, family members train one another to behave in dysfunctional ways in and out of the family situation. They train each other to be demanding, to behave in inappropriate and destructive ways, to be immature, and to be helpless. In short, all functional and dysfunctional behaviors in a family are a result of faulty training of one another by individual family members. They must be taught to identify and change these behaviors on a daily basis.

Key Words and Phrases

Operant conditioning
Personality
Environment
Reinforcement
Kinds of reinforcement
Levels of reinforcement
Social reinforcement
Punishment

THERAPEUTIC PROCESS

General Behavioristic Theory

The application of behavioristic principles to the treatment of human problems has been generally referred to as behavior modification or behavioral therapy. There are numerous adaptions of behaviorally oriented therapy; each are somewhat dependent on the training and experience of the therapist and on the population that he is serving. A behavior modification program used in a community mental health clinic serving primarily adults will necessarily differ from that used in a school classroom situation. However, these different adaptions share some common characteristics. It is my purpose here to present a general counseling process and common techniques that any behavioral therapist could use in his treatment. He may choose to alter one or more of the steps in the process or utilize slightly different techniques, but basically he would be operating from the position that I will outline in the next few pages.

It is possible to identify and describe at least four distinct steps in a behaviorist counseling process. The steps are sequential and interdependent. Data gathered in the first step will determine the content of the second and third stages. Hence, each step has critical tasks to accomplish that will eventually determine the success or failure of the entire process. The first step is principally involved with data gathering. A brief case history may be used to identify the antecedents of present day behavior and to discover clients' typical ways of responding in certain situations. This data gathering may be a formal assessment using a questionaire, personal history form, and selected diagnostic instruments. It may also be a rather informal interview situation with few prescribed procedures. The essence of this first step is to collect enough information in order to construct a complete and accurate picture of the individual and his environment. Whether this is done formally or informally is up to the discretion of the therapist.

The second step is based directly on the data gathered in the previous stage. The therapist identifies specific situations in the life of the client that are in need of remediation. Usually, the client plays an integral part in this identification process and agrees with the conclusions and plans of the therapist. On occasion, a therapist may choose to alter selected behaviors without the prior knowledge and consent of the individual. This is usually done only in exceptional situations and for sound professional reasons. The vast majority of treatment decisions are mutually shared by the client and the therapist.

The third step in the process is the development of the intervention program. Once all the appropriate data has been gathered about the individual and specific remediative situations have been identified, the therapist designs the intervention program. He wants to first get an indication of the strength of the behavior. How long has it been occurring and how often is it repeated? The frequency and duration of behaviors may determine the extent of the intervention. The measurement may be conducted by a third party or by the individual himself. Checklists and charts are commonly used to simplify and objectify this quantification of behavior. Behaviorists refer to the establishment of a baseline measurement before actual treatment begins. The next task is to choose the appropriate techniques and reinforcers that will be used to affect change. The behavioral therapist has a repertoire of methods that he can use with the most appropriate reinforcers for each client. A number of common techniques that behaviorists use will be presented later in this discussion. The intervention program is then put into continuous operation. Close monitoring of the program by the therapist is essential in the initial phases. The first several days may be critical to the overall effectiveness of the program. If changes are needed in any part of the intervention process, they must be accomplished as soon as possible. Many well-designed modification programs fail to alter behavior because the therapist did not closely monitor the client's reactions in the early phases of the program, and did not make the needed changes.

The fourth step in the therapeutic process is a follow-up of the case at selected intervals. Once the desired changes have occurred and the mutual goals have been reached, the therapeutic relationship is terminated. However, many behaviorists believe that periodic follow-up of specific clients is an integral part of the final phase of therapy. They want to check on the success of their efforts, and also to determine if any further intervention is necessary.

In summary, the following are the four steps in the process:

1. Data gathering
2. Identifying specific remediative situations
3. Development of the intervention program
   a. measure strength of behavior
   b. design the interventions
   c. institute the program
   d. periodically evaluate
4. Follow-up

As we have seen, the third step in the process is concerned with the intervention program itself. A critical element at this point is the selection of the most appropriate technique(s) for each client. There are a number of techniques that the therapist can choose. Some are more appropriate than others for treating selected kinds of behavior. Generally, they can be divided into two categories: those used to increase behavior and those that effectively decrease the strength of behavior. Four of the most popular methods used to increase desired behaviors are respondent conditioning, shaping, schedules of reinforcement, and modeling.

Respondent conditioning refers to the continuous, 100 percent reinforcement of behavior. It involves the immediate reinforcement of the selected behavior every time it occurs. The ease and effectiveness of this procedure has been demonstrated in laboratory situations with animals for many years. In less controlled environments with humans, it is a less viable technique to maintain. In many instances, it is impossible to reinforce every time. When using this technique, the therapist may have to settle for almost 100 percent reinforcement. Respondent conditioning is recommended for use when a new behavior is being learned. Because of its constant immediate nature it can cause a behavior to occur more rapidly and at a stronger rate than a less intensive reinforcement schedule.

Shaping is the process of rewarding successive approximation of a desired behavior. It is used when a behavior is not occurring or when a total behavioral response is unlikely to occur. The therapist rewards any approximation to the desired behavior. For instance, when teaching a child to read, a teacher will reward many approximations over several years before the total response of reading is achieved. An adult learning a new skill can be rewarded for achieving greater levels of mastery. Dieting and stopping smoking are also examples of the shaping technique.

Schedules of reinforcement is the third technique for increasing behavior. They involve the intermittent reinforcement of behavior on a planned basis. They can overcome some of the disadvantages of respondent conditioning. There are four different types of schedules that can be used.

1. *Fixed interval* — The subject is reinforced after a predetermined length of time in which the behavior has been occurring at a regular rate. Receiving a paycheck at two week intervals is a common example of this type of schedule.

2. *Variable interval* — This type is similar to the first,

except that the length of the interval is changeable.

3. Fixed ratio — Reinforcement occurs after a predetermined and consistent number of responses. An individual who is paid for piece work on an assembly line is on this type of reinforcement pattern.

4. Variable ratio — Again, reinforcement is given after a certain number of behavioral responses. However, the amount varies with each set of responses. Gambling machines are examples of this type of pattern. At one time, an individual might be rewarded for ten responses. The next time, the number could increase to twenty-five, and so on.

The last technique that we will discuss is modeling. It is essentially imitative learning that involves the copying of one person's behavior by another. An individual, verbally or nonverbally, displays a given behavior that is then repeated by a second person. It is one of the most common ways for adults and children to learn new behaviors in the environment. When used as a therapeutic technique, the counselor arranges for appropriate models to be observed and imitated by the client. Films, video tapes, novels, and television are common sources of observational learning.

The second category of reinforcement techniques are those that are used to decrease the strength of behaviors. The therapist may wish to completely erradicate a problem behavior in a client. To do this, he could choose one of the following five popular techniques developed for this purpose: extinction, satiation, punishment, time-out procedures, and systematic desensitization.

Extinction is simply the complete removal of reinforcement for a behavior. When a response occurs, it is ignored as a source of reward or gratification. Parents frequently use this technique to decrease a child's temper tantrums. Satiation refers to the process of overloading an individual with reinforcement. The rewards are so overwhelming to an individual that he chooses to stop responding in order to avoid the reinforcement. What was once a pleasure reward is now an aversive situation that must be terminated. This technique is not considered to be as effective or efficient as the other four.

A third technique for decreasing behavior is punishment. It is basically an attempt to suppress or inhibit an unwanted behavior. Punishment can take many forms. It can be as subtle as a frown or as blatant as a slap in the face. The overall effectiveness of this technique is a hotly debated issue in behavioral circles. Some of the pros and cons of its use were discussed in the previous section. The fourth technique, time-out procedures, was also discussed in the previous section. Briefly stated, time-out is the removal of an individual from a reinforcing situation in order to eliminate his unwanted responses. It is widely used in clinics, hospitals, industrial, and school settings.

The final most commonly used procedure to decrease behavior is systematic desensitization. This procedure was developed by Joseph Wolpe and is widely used to treat anxiety and phobic complaints. It involves the gradual pairing of an anxiety-producing situation with the relaxed state of the client.

By following the four step process and incorporating one or more of the techniques into the intervention program, the therapist can quickly and efficiently begin to change behavior. This behavioristic approach is effective with individuals, small groups, classroom-size groups, and large groups of subjects.

Social Learning Approach

The Social Learning Approach uses the basic behavioral therapy principles that have been discussed and focuses them on the family unit. Essentially, the therapy program consists of the family itself putting behavioral principles into action. It is important for family members to realize that they can change their own and each other's behavior by systematically applying learning theory principles. The therapist asks himself several key questions at the beginning of therapy. What are individuals in this family teaching themselves and others? How are they reinforcing each other in functional and dysfunctional interactions? What are they willing to do about their current situation?

The counseling program that Patterson advocates is similar to the general behavioristic program. It does not necessarily have to be as complex and structured as the process that was presented. But even a casual family program contains the same elements as a highly organized program in an institutional setting. The first step in a family program is for the individuals to decide what behavior(s) they want to change. Patterson feels that if an undesireable behavior is to be removed or decreased there should also be planned reinforcement of a new desireable behavior to replace it. In other words, the family is focusing on two behaviors: one to replace the other.

The second step is to count and record the target behavior(s). A baseline measurement, taken over several days, may be necessary in order for the family to get a feeling for the strength of the unwanted behavior. The Social Learning Approach advocates the use of charts and graphs as an efficient and systematic way to gather the initial data.

Establishing the program is the third step. The family must decide specifically what it is that is going to happen in their unit. Goals are established, and several techniques are chosen as the most appropriate for the specific situation. Social reinforcers are the favorite choice of the therapist in this model. All desirable behavior must be reinforced as frequently and as immediately as possible. In behavioristic terminology, use respondent conditioning as a first choice. When this is not possible, use some variation of a reinforcement schedule. If individuals are trying to teach a complex behavior, shaping is the preferred technique. We can't expect people to immediately form complex behaviors that involve many stages. Children, particularly, must be taught new behaviors in gradual increments. Modeling is another effective technique that can be used in the Social Learning Approach.

To decrease or eliminate unwanted behaviors, the use of natural consequences are a preferred choice. Time-out procedures are also commonly recommended by this model. Punishment is not recommended in any situation. If it must be used, then individuals should apply only mildly aversive stimuli to decrease a specific behavior. Patterson advocates the use of contracts between family members as an effective device to increase and decrease behaviors. They can provide a way of eliciting a commitment from the individuals involved and can also help to structure a casual family program.

Once the program is in operation, the family should continue to count and record behavior. This can provide a continuous progress report, and it can also act as a social reinforcer for the new behavior. Periodic changes in the initial program may have to be made in order to deal with unforeseen occurrances. The family should be prepared to do this and not view program changes as an indication of faulty techniques or poor planning. When the new behavior is learned and/or the old behavior is eliminated, the program is gradually phased out. Ideally, the family has internalized the new ways of interacting, and their goals have been reached.

The therapeutic process, in most cases, is short-term. It is nonanalytical and focuses primarily on overt and observable behaviors. Advocates of behavioristic approaches feel that these qualities provide a distinct advantage for their model over other popular therapy models. Whether this is valid or not is for the individual therapist to decide. However, behavioral therapy is the treatment of choice for an ever growing number of students and experienced clinicians on the international scene.

Key Words and Phrases

Behavior modification
Steps in the process
Data gathering
Baseline measurement
Respondent conditioning
Shaping
Schedules of reinforcement
Modeling
Extinction
Satiation
Time-out procedures
Systematic desensitization
Charts and graphs
Natural consequences
Contracts

CHAPTER 5

INTEGRATIVE MODEL

DESCRIPTION OF MAJOR THEORIST

William M. Walsh, Ph.D.

Professional Positions. Professor, Northeastern Illinois University. Psychologist, Northbrook, Illinois. Consultant, Northbrook, Illinois.

Major Publication. *Counseling Children and Adolescents.* Berkeley, California, McCutchan Publishing Corporation, 1975.

INTRODUCTION TO THEORY

INTEGRATIVE Family Therapy is the product of my own personal and professional experiences from the past and in the present day. It is a result of a continuing process of growth, development, and maturity. Mine is a similar process to that experienced by most, if not all, professional theorists and practicioners in every field of endeavor. It is a process that must be initiated and endured by every student of a skilled occupation or professional discipline. My specific experiences may be different from other people undergoing this process, but the process itself is essentially the same. Most readers of this text will find it easy to identify with the process that I am alluding to. Because the product is a result of the influence and ideas of others, it is not unique to me and does not contain any startling breakthroughs in the field of counseling and psychology. It is an integration of the thinking and practice of selected others with my own personal background. It is my own personal framework of therapy that I use in my helping relationships.

My first introduction to therapy was through the traditional individual models of counseling and psychotherapy. Further professional training emphasized these individual models and gradually incorporated concepts and skills from the group therapy movement. This blending of individual and group models led naturally to my interest and subsequent immersion in the theories of family therapy. For me, family therapy is a logical extension of the individual and group counseling theories. It provides for me the most powerful methods for dealing with the human problem situations that I encounter in my professional work. However, I still rely on the concepts of individual personality development in order to understand the complexities of family living. This combination of the concepts of individual personality with the theories of family therapy is expressed in my work as Integrative Family Therapy. It is an integration of several models of family therapy and the traditional ideas of individual personality dynamics.

The treatment population that a therapist serves is largely dictated by his geographic location and his employment setting. A counselor working in a deprived inner city location will be serving a clientele that is necessarily different than if he was located in an affluent neighborhood or suburb. Therapists in private practice are frequently confronted with client complaints that are different from those seen in public counseling agencies. In this sense, our patient population can dictate the way we as therapists develop our ideas about the origins of personal problems and the strategies that we use in treating these difficulies. My treatment population, seen in a private treatment setting, consists mainly of middle class families and couples who are motivated to remove the pain and conflict from their immediate situation. They see outside intervention as a potentially positive source of relief and growth for all concerned.

Most therapists that I know find themselves working with a relatively homogeneous client population. Experienced counselors can identify the most common syndromes that they treat and they can expect certain presenting problems to occur with regularity. I have identified four general problem situations that I encounter in the people that I serve. One or more of these problems is observable in the vast majority of my treatment population. They are not the only problems that are treated, of course, but since they occur so frequently they can provide initial insights into the particular family in question.

The most common major problem that I see in families is a lack of responsibility in fulfilling role expectations. This irresponsibility can be present in any or all family members regardless of age or position in the unit. In one family, it might be the parents who are not providing adequate structure or limits for their children. They may be over-indulging the children or not requiring them to follow thru with age appropriate tasks. Mother may expect her children to clean their rooms, pick-up their clothes, and take out the garbage, but there is little or no follow-through on her part if these things are not done. The expectations for fulfilling certain tasks are present, but she is not teaching them how to complete these tasks on a regular basis. This type of parent will often come to the therapist in a state of frustration and despair. He or she cannot understand why the children are not doing the things that are expected of them. They are irresponsible children. Close inspection of the dynamics of the situation reveal a different picture, however. Rather than the children being irresponsible, it is the parents who have not structured and taught their children to complete tasks. They, the parents, are the irresponsible ones in the family, and they need to learn how to control and motivate their children.

The lack of follow-through and motivation in the children at home can easily carry over into the school situation. Classroom teachers are familiar with many children who have poor work habits, who are disorganized, and who appear to be unmotivated. They may well be a product of this type of home environment. Families who are referred by educational institutions for therapy are the most apt to present this problem orientation. In another family, the irresponsibility of the parents could manifest itself in lack of financial or emotional support. Either or both of the parents may be so uninvolved or occupied elsewhere that there is little parental input into the unit. Their contacts with the children may consist only of negative comments, commands, or punishments. Irresponsible parenting of this type can be seen in every socioeconomic level and every type of living arrangement.

The second most common problem that I encounter in families is poor communication and/or perception. The topic of communication and perception will be discussed in greater detail in the next section. For our purposes here, I will briefly define the terms and give examples of how this problem is usually presented in therapy. Communication is the sending of a message in any verbal, nonverbal, or extrasensory manner. Perception is the receiving of that message. To me, they are two separate processes and must be treated as such. A family member may send a very clear concise message to another but it may be perceived in a very distorted way. The problem in this case is not with the sender but with the receiver. The therapeutic implications are quite different depending on the source of the clarity or distortion. If the communication itself is unclear and confusing, it is impossible to have healthy perception. In this latter case, the focus of intervention is on communication and not just perception. Usually, a family with this core problem is unaware of the dynamics of the situation. The husband may feel he is communicating exactly what he is feeling, and he can't understand why his wife is not responding appropriately to him. Mother may feel she is making her wishes perfectly clear to her family, and she is frustrated when her requests are not acceded to. In each case, there is a problem with communication, perception, or both. By separating the two processes, the therapist can focus on the specific difficulty more readily and effect change more expeditiously.

Unrealistic expectations are the third most common family syndrome that I see in therapy. This problem is closely related to role irresponsibility, but may not contain any aspects of irresponsibility. Family members may be religiously fulfilling their roles, but they may be unhappy and dissatisfied with the results of their labor. The problem in this case is not completion of tasks, but rather unrealistically high expectations of accomplishment. Most of us are familiar with parents who set very high standards for themselves and their children. They appear to have many of the good things in life; yet they express considerable dissatisfaction with their lot in life. This general syndrome can have many specific expressions in each family member. Father may be constantly nagging the children about their academic progress or their social life. The children may turn to alcohol or drugs or drop out of school and society. The anxious impulsive child can also be a result of overly high parental expectations. All family members can internalize unrealistic expectations and develop their own way of expressing or coping with the concommitant frustration and anxiety.

The fourth most common problem is parental discord. This disharmony is usually chronic and generalized to the total relationship. However, it can be specific to several major personal or family issues. Lack of agreement about child discipline, academic progress, or financial issues are examples of specific topics that can create tension and pressure in a family. Left unresolved, specific issues can be as destructive as generalized parental unhappiness. The tension and pressure that is generated by continual parental disagreements spreads quickly to other family members. One or more of the children may act out the tension or it may be expressed as an overall family frustration and depression. The specific daily results may be quite different, but the source of the difficulty lies in the parental relationship.

Seldom are these four core problems seen in isolation. Usually at least two are in combination with each other or other presenting problems. Whatever the presenting problem(s), for me the treatment of choice is Integrative Family Therapy. The remaining two sections of this chapter will deal with the specific concepts and treatment procedures of this model. Most of them should be familiar to you since they have been garnered from theories of individual, group, and family therapy and integrated into the following model.

THEORY OF PERSONALITY

Most therapy models focus on abnormal, deviant, or dysfunctional behavior. The concepts of theories are developed to describe these behaviors and to treat them. Little, if any, space is allotted for a discussion of healthy functioning. This type of presentation is particularly well suited for therapists who work primarily with clinical or psychiatric populations. It is less appropriate for those of us who work mainly with the less deviant, "normal" range of problems. Most nonpsychiatric, outpatient therapy is conducted with people who can function in society, but who wish to change aspects of themselves that are limiting their functioning or are making them unhappy. This type of client population does not need periodic hospitalization, drug treatment, or major personality change. Since much of family therapy falls into this category, I find it helpful to start from a position of describing healthy functioning. Once the primary aspects of a well-functioning family are identified, deviations from that norm can be isolated and treated.

In order to be considered well-functioning, there are a number of tasks that a family must fulfill. The following is a list of those that I consider to be most critical for the healthy development of the family. The reader may wish to add several more.

1. Teaching/learning
2. Support
3. Stability
4. Mutuality/privacy
5. Independence/dependence
6. Defining expectations
7. Problem solving

One of the most important is the teaching/learning task. Traditionally, the family has been the major vehicle for communicating all forms of knowledge and skills. The parents or grandparents are the first teachers that a child encounters. The learning process begins in early infancy. These may seem like simple statements that do not need to be stated. However, we find in our society that parents are doing less teaching and relying on other institutions in society to relay the critical growth messages. Parents are confused about what they should be saying to or doing with their children, and many can be easily swayed by new trends or pseudo experts. As children mature, they teach their parents new ideas and new ways of behaving. A shared teaching/learning process can develop among all family members that promotes growth and change. The openness and mutuality of teaching/learning can be a good barometer of the state of health of a family.

A second task of the family unit is to provide support for its individual members. Steady financial support is basic to the continuing growth of all members, yet emotional support and encouragement is equally important. An absence of either can promote insecurity and be the prime source of debilitating anxiety in both adults and children. A closely related yet separate task is the provision of stability in family relationships. Set patterns of behavior for all family members can give structure in a confusing and changeable world. Children like to know when their father or mother will be away or at home. Regular routines by parents are a source of security for kids. A permanent living arrangement, set times for going to bed and arising, consistent meal times, and seasonal traditions are all ways of providing stability in a family situation. Rigid, compulsive behaviors are not encouraged either. Periodic variations of routine are healthy and invigorating. However, consistent and reliable support and stability are two of the major ways of promoting a feeling of security and safety in all family members.

Two other closely related tasks are the promotion of mutuality/privacy and the development of independence. Mutuality refers to the process of a family working together for common goals. Each member knows that they can depend on others for help in time of need. Yet each member needs his or her private time and space to grow individually and apart from the unit. This is particularly true of the adolescent, but all family members need a place and a time to call their own. Private possessions, that do not have to be shared, can give a child a feeling of uniqueness and individuality. Members can be themselves, yet feel a part of and work toward the growth of the entire family. The encouragement of independence in a family is crucial for the gradual development of a healthy self-concept for each person. Children must be taught and encouraged to function on their own and to be dependent only on themselves in certain situations. This process can begin in early childhood with age appropriate behaviors. A child can be given chores that he must complete alone. A child of four might be expected to dress himself everyday. At six years, he might be expected to take reasonable care of his toys. By ten years of age, he could be expected to make a contribution to the care and maintenance of the home. Chores that are geared to the age of the child can give him a feeling of self-importance and worth. As the child matures, he can be given more responsibilities and decisions. This process results in the gradual development of independent behaviors and adultlike reactions. An independent and mutually functioning person is the eventual goal.

The sixth task, defining expectations, was briefly discussed in the preceding section. Setting unrealistic expectations for individuals or the unit are a source of conflict and unhappiness. However, the establishment of reasonable short-term and long-term goals are essential for orderly, planned development. The emphasis here is on reasonable. What can people rationally expect from themselves and others on a daily and yearly basis? Is there a good chance that the goals will be reached? In this context, reasonable expectations refer to those that are acceptable to all concerned and that have a good chance of being accomplished. This is more likely to occur in a family atmosphere of open discussion and mutual decision making. All family members should feel free to affirm or negate, accept or reject, establish and change personal and family expectations. This is of course a continuous process that requires considerable commitment from all involved.

The final task is specifically concerned with the problem-solving process that is present in each person and every unit. The key question is, how are problems defined and resolved in the immediate present? Is it a rigid process that tolerates little or no new input? Or, is it a flexible process that seeks out new data in an attempt to find new solutions or alternatives? The way a family handles insignificant daily problems is a key to how they attempt to deal with important conflicts. Flexibility and openness are the prime ingredients in a satisfying problem-solving process. Much of what happens in family therapy revolves around helping people to establish and maintain a rewarding problem-solving approach to living. In this sense, the remainder of this chapter will be devoted to that topic.

Family Growth Process

It might be helpful at this point in our discussion to examine how problems develop in a family and how they are handled in functional and dysfunctional ways. It is possible to identify a family growth process and to chart in a general way the healthy and unhealthy directions a family chooses in the process. Structure 8 and the following description is my way of conceptualizing this process.

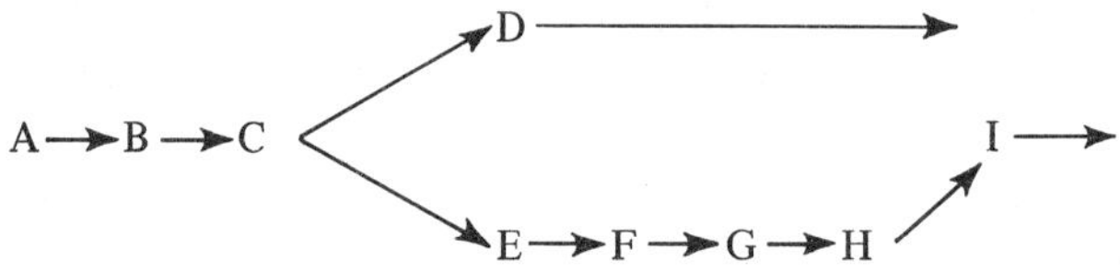

Structure 8

A. Two individuals come together and form a relationship. This relationship usually involves a marriage commitment. Each of these people brings their own background from their family of origin and their own individual personality dynamics to the relationship.

B. From the very beginning, this relationship develops its own dynamics and characteristics. In other words, they develop methods for dealing with one another in an intimate situation, and create joint ways of interacting with the outside world. Eventually, this couple may have children, which broadens the number of possible interactions in the new family.

C. The natural maturation and aging process of individuals in the unit produces conflict and strain. In the process of daily living, individual members interact among themselves and with the outside world, which also produces stress. They attempt to cope with the stress and resolve the conflict on the basis of "A," "B," and new data that is acquired from the outside world. All of the above sources may be appropriate and functional, or they may be distorted and dysfunctional.

D. If the family has established a functional process, i.e. appropriate "A," "B," and new data, they will deal with the stress and conflict and achieve resolution. They are then free to continue with daily living in a satisfying way.

E. Dysfunction results when a family does not have a healthy process. The immediate stress or conflict is not resolved, and unfinished feelings may linger and interrupt daily living.

F. Frequently, families perpetuate the dysfunction by refusing to change (rigid problem solving) or by not knowing alternatives that may be available to them.

G. Dysfunction is eventually expressed in one or more of the individuals in the family. The unhealthy process has occurred for years, and the unit is no longer capable of containing the stress and pressure. It is at this point that a professional would enter the picture. The family may seek help on their own. It is more likely, however, that another institution in society will notice their difficulties and refer them for treatment. Educational institutions or law enforcement agencies are frequently the first to notice disruption in a family or an individual member, hence they are prime referral agents for therapy. The family may refuse to recognize the problem or to seek professional help. In this instance, it is likely that their problems will continue and perhaps intensify. Spontaneous recovery is highly unlikely.

H. If the family chooses to seek professional help, the therapeutic intervention process begins. Ideally, the professional identifies the dysfunction and helps the family to make remediative changes. This may be a short-range or a long-term process. They develop new ways of relating to one another, new problem solving methods, and a greater understanding of themselves and others.

I. After termination of therapy, the family can now meet and resolve future stress and conflict.

The family growth process described above is, of course, theoretical. But it can give the therapist a feeling for what happens to a family when they are experiencing difficulty, where therapy enters the picture, and what can be expected as a result of intervention. It is important to note that much has happened to a family prior to therapeutic intervention. Frequently, the therapist efforts are viewed by the family as a "last ditch effort" to make their family right. It can be helpful for the family to realize that years of dysfunctional interaction cannot be changed overnight. Much time and effort must be expended in some cases to produce satisfying results. It can be a long and difficult road from "C" to "I," but the results can seem worthwhile if a family can picture themselves at "D" or "I" for the rest of their lives.

General Characteristics of Families

In order to identify functional and dysfunctional aspects of families, it is necessary to discuss characteristics that all families have in common. These characteristics are the ways and the means that all families attempt to carry out their functions and meet their stated and unstated goals. I will start my presentation with general characteristics that I consider to be universal in families, and conclude with specific characteristics that relate directly to health and illness in individuals and family groupings. The following five broad statements should give the reader a feeling for the philosophical position of Integrative Family Therapy.

The family is a system. It is a network of specific interrelated and interdependent parts. Each person in the family, as well as groupings of people are parts of the whole. Each individual is a separate part by virtue of his being a member. But he is also another part of the whole each time he joins with another member of members in a subgrouping. For example, the father is one part because he is an individual in the unit. But he is also a second part because he is in the parent subgrouping. He may also be other parts when he joins other individuals in subgroupings. In other words, each family member is at least one part and probably more than one in each family unit. The natural process of growth and development causes each part to change. Even a slight change in any one part necessitates a change or realignment in other parts. One can imagine the ramifications in a system if any one of its parts experiences major change. The therapist must be especially attuned to the multiplicity of parts and the potential or actual consequences of change if he is to truly understand and monitor the innerworkings of the unit.

A family is significantly influenced by aspects of its unique heredity and environment. Heredity refers to all innate biological elements of the person that are transmitted via the genes of the parent. The environment is composed of all factors, besides genetic elements, that influence the growth and development of the individual. Since each person responds differently to environmental influences, each member of the family has his own unique composition of environmental factors. In other words, no two people in the family internalize the same factors in any given situation. Because environmental aspects are continually influencing an individual from intrauterine life to death, they are considered to be more important than inherited elements of the person.

All behaviors, attitudes, values, and feelings can be both rational (enhancing) or irrational (dysfunctional) to the individual or the family system. The context or situation in which they are expressed is the determining factor. In one situation, a child's overt aggressive behaviors may be totally inappropriate and considered to be unhealthy, e.g. in the classroom. The same behavior in a different context might be interpreted as an appropriate response, e.g. in an athletic contest. The key point is that behaviors, attitudes, values, and feelings do not possess inherent worth in and of themselves. They are not judged to be good or bad out of context. The total situation must be taken into consideration when an evaluation is made. An individual's seemingly bizarre behavior may be an appropriate response to his particular family situation at that point in time. The same might be said for a total family's reactions to their environment. What on the surface may seem to be irrational and dysfunctional may be an appropriate adaptional response. The therapist must avoid labeling or being judgemental without a close evaluation of the total situation. Behaviors, attitudes, values, and feelings cannot be adequately understood out of context.

Homeostasis is a desired state for all individuals and systems. As needs arise, tension is produced in the organism. The satisfaction of those needs reduces the tension and returns the system to a more balanced even state. This is an ideal situation in which needs are appropriately satisfied and a comfortable balance is achieved. When needs are left unsatisfied, the tension remains in the system. Homeostasis is not achieved, and the organism must find other ways of returning to the balanced state. Frequently, these other ways are dysfunctional because they do not lead to the satisfaction of the original need. Their goal is to reduce tension, not satisfy needs. Neuroses and psychoses are common ways for individuals to achieve a temporary balance without actually satisfying the original need. Symptoms like phobias, conversion reactions, and depression are an individual's own homeostatic mechanism. A common balance mechanism for a family is to project the tension in the unit onto one of the members. Instead of the entire system being upset, unbalanced, it is an individual who is behaving in inappropriate ways. Whether it is occurring in an individual or in a system, the homeostatic mechanism is always dysfunctional since it can never achieve the ideal goal of need satisfaction. At best, it can only achieve a temporary unnatural reduction of tension. The tendency of individuals and families to trigger the homeostatic mechanism and to achieve balance at all costs must be continually countered by the therapist. The tension is necessary to keep the organism searching for appropriate satisfaction of its needs. The homeostatic mechanism will only postpone or temporarily avoid this quest.

All behaviors of an individual or a system are attempts to preserve and enhance the organism. The goal is never to destroy. The result may be self-destructive, but the intent is always growth. With this in mind, all debilitating and harmful behaviors, attitudes, values, and feelings are distorted or misdirected attempts to save or to help the system. In other words, no organism has the capacity to willfully and knowingly produce self-destruction.

Specific Characteristics of Families

The following five specific characteristics are based on the preceding philosophical position of Integrative Family Therapy. They are the means that the therapist uses in developing his diagnostic picture of the family and each individual member. This evaluation should lead to an individualized treatment plan for the family, which will consist of treatment goals, working hypotheses, and intervention strategies. Everything that is done in therapy should relate directly to these five specific characteristics.

Individual Personality Dynamics

Personality dynamics refer to those strategies that an individual uses to organize, understand, and complete the tasks of daily living. They are the overt and covert means that a person uses for need satisfaction. Some of these ways will be functional and lead to a personal feeling of comfort and well-being, i.e. tension reduction. Other dynamics are dysfunctional because they distort or avoid reality in an attempt to attain immediate tension relief and also fail to satisfy the original need.

Students of individual therapy models are familiar with the various explanations that theorists use to explain behavior. Psychoanalytic literature gives us one of the most well-developed and accepted theories for understanding behavior. Neoanalytic writers have expanded on the thinking of Freud and have produced an impressive array of concepts for explaining human behavior. I find neoanalytic explanations of defense mechanisms to be particularly helpful in my work However, the reader may choose from any one of a number of other theoretical models. The important factor is that the Integrative Family therapist have specific concepts for understanding individual behavior that are complementary to the concepts of family dynamics. Several of the major models that I feel blend well with the Integrative approach are Adlerian Psychology, Rational Emotive Therapy, Reality Therapy, and Gestalt Therapy. The particular model chosen is less important than the fact that the therapist has a model for understanding behavior.

When the therapist begins to analyze individual personality dynamics, it is the parents who should be considered first. They are the architects of this family and have in a sense created some of the personality dynamics of their children. They are also the carriers of the dynamics from their own family origins. For instance, the Father's way of dealing with aggressive male behavior may be different from his wife's because of the different circumstances of their development. Much parental behavior can be understood from an analysis of individual personality dynamics that were internalized by the husband and wife in their own family. These personality dynamics are then used in the current family for the development of family dynamics. They are transmitted to the children who in turn develop their own individual strategies for coping with each other and the outside world.

It is the position of Integrative Family Therapy that individual personality dynamics alone are inadequate for understanding and explaining the myriad of forces that affect family life. However, they are an important ingredient in the mix of interpersonal relationships. As such, they are an essential piece of the entire family puzzle.

Family Subsystems (Subunits)

A subsystem is any grouping in a family that consists of one or more individuals who unite for a particular purpose or to share a common bond. Some subsystems are related to chronological age. The most common of these are the parental subsystem and the sibling subsystem. The children's subsystem can further divide according to age, sex, or common interests. The parents also form another subunit called the marital subsystem. Since the marital and parental subsystems have different tasks and require different behaviors, it is important to separate the two theoretically and in daily living. Any number of subunits or combinations is possible in a given family. Even a family with an only child is considered to have a sibling subsystem consisting of one.(For a more thorough explanation of subsystems refer to the chapter on Structural Family Therapy.)

Roles of Individuals in the Family

For our purpose, a role is defined as the identity that a family member assumes, on a temporary or permanent basis, in order to complete certain tasks. In many instances, they involve specific duties that must be performed on a regular schedule. Since the completion of tasks is essential for a family to fulfill its various functions, appropriate role definition and follow-through is a particularly critical characteristic. Roles, tasks, and functions are considered to be appropriate when they follow a certain sequence of events similar to the following. Individual roles are clearly defined and articulated by the family. All members contribute to the definitions and accept their assigned duties. All members assume the responsibility for fulfilling their particular role. When roles are fulfilled, tasks are completed. The completion of tasks leads to the fulfillment of family functions.

> Appropriate role = completed tasks = fulfilled functions = growth and development of indviduals, subgroups, and the entire unit.

This sequence is critical for healthy adoption and change in a family. A breakdown in role definition or responsibility will make it difficult, if not impossible, to eventually fulfill family functions. At the very least, individuals will be dissatisfied with their own or others' behaviors. This is the specific characteristic that relates directly to one of the major problems that I discussed earlier, namely, role irresponsibility. Some parents feel that they are doing their children a favor by not giving them age appropriate duties, or by not requiring them to follow-through on assigned tasks. By not doing these things, they are raising pampered, irresponsible children. This attitude usually carries over into the classroom and to social activities. Another contributing factor to role irresponsibility is the lack of clearly defined and articulated roles for family members. Certain behaviors may be assumed or taken for granted without ever being clearly articulated. In other words, people don't know what they should be doing or how they should be doing it. Any or all members can be placed in this position. Mother may not know what her husband considers a "good wife." She may do what she considers best, but is frustrated and unhappy by her husband's negative reactions. Parental attitudes about child rearing fall into this category. Another, more insidious problem with roles involves the ascribing of individual roles, labeling individuals, or scapegoating family members. By definition, labeling, ascribing, and scapegoating involve lack of consent on the part of the individual. A role is given to him, and he is expected to accept it and follow through without choice or input. This situation is one of the most resistant to change in therapy.

Generally speaking, role irresponsibility is a result of one or more of the following:

a. incomplete role definition
b. poorly articulated roles
c. lack of personal input of consensus concerning individual roles
d. inconsistent completion of duties
e. ascribing, labeling, or scapegoating

Family Themes

A theme is defined as any issue in a family that occurs frequently and absorbs a significant amount of interest and attention of family members. These issues can be positive (growth enhancing) or they can be negative (counterproductive, destructive). Positive themes involve the family in constructive activities and can lead to growth for all involved. They are characterized by an early resolution of conflict and a healthy channeling of tension to accomplish certain goals. Family athletic pursuits, intellectual or cultural activities, and home maintenance are common examples of positive themes. Negative themes, on the other hand, are characterized by the nonresolution of conflict and increased tension. Whenever the issue surfaces in the family, it creates disharmony and unhappiness. Common examples of negative themes would include unsatisfactory academic achievement, role irresponsibility, differences in child rearing practices, and generational attitudes about individual behaviors.

All families have several identifiable major themes. They occur on a regular basis and each usually involves the same dynamics every time. It would be like listening to the same record played many times. The family is caught in a rigid pattern and forced to replay the same sequence, particularly in the case of negative themes. They have little choice in how they will behave and seek few alternatives. In the case of positive themes, the family may choose to respond in a similar fashion each time the issue occurs. The difference is that they choose the behaviors because they bring pleasure and growth. They are not forced into patterns because of rigidity or the absence of alternatives.

The therapist should attempt to identify the major positive or negative themes as soon as possible. Usually, several themes surface in the first two sessions. They may be negative and hence can generate the initial therapeutic goals for change. They may involve the things that trouble the family the most on a daily basis, and their resolution can give the family greater hope for continued change. In other words, the resolution of initial themes positively disposes the family to work on other more resistant problems. The feeling of relief that short-term change can produce may lead the family to premature termination. The therapist must be aware of this and work to counteract it from the first session. Also, positive themes should not be ignored or forgotten. It is important for the family to see the positive aspects of themselves while they are working to resolve the negative themes.

Communication and Perception

Communication and perception is perhaps the most important of all of the others and a key element in all interpersonal relationships. Every human overt and covert behavior involves communication and perception. We cannot survive in the world at any level of existence without communicating and perceiving on a moment-to-moment basis. None of the other characteristics can operate to their maximum capacities without accurate and clear communication and perception. Since they are so vitally important, they are the eventual focus of almost every therapeutic encounter. The counselor may initially choose to realign subgroups in a family or create greater role responsibility or resolve a negative theme. But eventually, communication and perception will be an item of discussion and possibly intensive intervention. In most cases, in order to maximize the fulfillment of functions, a family will need to make changes in their communication/perception process.

Communication, as previously stated, is the transmission of a message in any verbal, nonverbal, or extrasensory manner. It is one aspect of a two part process. Perception is the act of receiving that message. It is a different aspect of the process and must be considered separately when the therapist is evaluating the complete process. Clear communication is possible without accurate perception. But the reverse is very difficult to achieve. For example, one member can send a clear, distinct message accurately, while another receives a distorted message. The problem is not with the communicator, but with the perceiver. Hence, the focus of intervention is on the perceiver. Asking the communicator to change his method of transmitting may be ineffective or even counterproductive. The emphasis should be on more accurate perception by this one individual. On the other hand, if the problem is the transmission of mixed, double, or confused messages, then the focus of intervention is quite different.

Most families have consistent, characteristic methods of communication. They have an established process that varies little from incident to incident. If they are communicating inaccurately, it usually occurs the same way each time. In order to identify the patterns, the therapist can pose several questions. "How do people in the family communicate with one another?" "How do the family and individual members communicate with others outside of the family?" "What are the channels of communication?"

Individuals may communicate and perceive differently with their family than with outside sources. Differences can be seen more often with communication than with perception. Usually, if an individual is perceiving inaccurately with family members it is pervasive throughout all of his contacts. Accurate communication, on the other hand, can vary from situation to situation. Channels of communication refer to the individuals or groups that are usually involved in a situation. If the sibling subgroup is communicating with the parental, which parent is usually chosen? Or, are both chosen? When do they go to Dad? When do they go to Mom? Who handles communication with the school? Each situation may have to be explored depending on the major themes that are presented or on the roles that are established in the family. As the therapist and family interact, he can begin to pinpoint specific incidents and reorganize patterns in the therapy session. This reorganization usually occurs concurrently with other goals of therapy.

The preceding five specific characteristics represent the

working framework of the therapist from which all change strategies will emanate. All of the therapist's interactions with the family will be governed by the hypotheses that he generates from the specific characteristics. The way that he actualizes these theoretical formulations is the subject of the next Therapeutic Process section.

Key Words and Phrases

Family tasks	Individual homeostatic mechanism
Mutuality/privacy	Specific family characteristics
Problem-solving	Individual personality dynamics
Family growth process	Roles of individuals
General family characteristics	Family themes
Family homeostasis	Communication/perception process

THERAPEUTIC PROCESS

From a theoretical standpoint, therapy is a well-defined and structured process with specific stages that each have certain tasks to accomplish. The therapist organizes the therapeutic encounter according to these stages and tasks, and moves in an orderly fashion to successful termination. This type of theoretical process provides direction for the counselor and guideposts from which to evaluate the progress of the family. In actual practice, the process is less structured. Stages overlap and blend with one another as the flow of the session moves from person to person or from topic to topic. The therapist might move from stage one to stage two and into stage three in a matter of minutes. He may then have to circle back to stage one in order to complete a necessary structuring task. In other words, the reality of a session does not always fit the organized theoretical pattern. Even so, for the Integrative Family therapist, the theoretical pattern is essential to provide structure to a potentially disorganized and chaotic presentation of ideas, feelings, and behaviors. A family in conflict, under varying degrees of tension and anxiety, does not have the capacity to rationally evaluate what each member is saying, feeling, or doing and then to take steps to remediate the situation. The therapist, who has an organized theoretical process, has the capacity to impose order, establish goals, and chart future directions. The fact that he does not always adhere to a rigid theoretical pattern is irrelevant. The point is that he has the cognitive structure of a theoretical process to guide him in each individual session and in the entire therapeutic encounter with the family.

The theoretical therapeutic process of Integrative Family Therapy consists of five relatively distinct stages. Each stage has specific tasks that must be accomplished before the family can move completely to the next stage. In other words, the stages are developmental in that one prepares the family for the tasks in the next. The five stages are organized so that a family can progress in an orderly fashion to accomplish the two major goals of Integrative Family Therapy:

1. To remediate specific immediate difficulties and concerns of individuals and the family unit.
2. To build a satisfying problem-solving process that the family and individual members can use to deal with future problems.

These two goals reflect the twofold emphasis of Integrative Family Therapy. Of initial importance is the resolution of present difficulties that are sapping the day-to-day energies of the family. Setting and accomplishing short-term goals prepares and motivates the family to develop a more functional life long problem-solving orientation. Success in the present tense inspires confidence and trust in their future potential. The removal of pain and the reduction in conflict on a daily basis frees the family to devote more energy to long range plans. The two goals are present in the mind of the therapist from the first session and give him direction from week to week.

Stages in Therapy

Structuring

The therapist asserts his control from the beginning of the

first session. This is not an authoritarian type of situation. It is an encounter between a professional with certain skills and a group of individuals who seek his assistance regarding certain problem situations. It is a consultive type of relationship that is analogous to that of an architect and a home builder or an accountant and a client. The therapist is employed by the family to assist them in finding solutions to their individual and group problems. It is never a power or an adversary relationship. The professional, by virtue of his training and experience, has certain skills that are needed by the client. It is not a personal, social, or mystical relationship. In a sense, it is a businesslike arrangement that happens to involve intensely personal ideas, feelings, and behaviors. This is not to say that the therapist must be isolated and coldly analytical. On the contrary, mutual feelings of warmth, acceptance, and caring are essential for a productive therapeutic encounter. The therapist is in a unique and difficult position. He must maintain his objectivity and separateness, at the same time that he is inserting himself into the human drama of each family's lives. Establishing and maintaining this type of relationship is the first challenge of therapy. By exerting initial control, the therapist instills confidence in the family and optimism that change can occur. There is order and stability in their life, at least when they are in the session. The therapist's behavior also provides role models for individuals to emulate in the session and in their outside contacts.

In order to establish control and yet promote an accepting cooperative atmosphere, the counselor has several critical tasks to perform in the first session. First, he should be firm about the overt parameters of their contractual relationship. For instance, he should establish a set time and length for their first few sessions. Frequently, one and one-half hours is required for the first two or three weekly sessions, because of the structuring, organizing, and evaluating procedures that take place. After this, one hour sessions on a weekly or biweekly basis may be appropriate. The therapist should also request that all family members attend the first several sessions, so that he can observe how they interact, introduce the entire family to the counseling process, and gather information from all family members. Later sessions can involve any combination of individuals that the therapist deems necessary.

The general idea, again, is that the therapist sets the initial limits (without being dogmatic) for their relationship. A family may attempt to manipulate the counselor in these early stages and this may be symptomatic of their pathology. By being firm and consistent, the therapist can begin, very early, to restructure dysfunctional interactional behaviors. By vacillating, the therapist allows the family to control his behavior, and perhaps resist intervention at a later date.

The second critical task is to make contact with each individual member, and to elicit help and information from them. The therapist wants to communicate his concern for the family and his willingness to accept them no matter what develops in their relationship. The classic ideas about therapeutic rapport are relevant at this point. Trust, acceptance, confidentiality, and unconditional positive regard are feelings that the therapist can communicate to each member in order to build the rapport. Each individual should be led to feel that they are important to the success of the relationship and that whatever they say is important to the counselor. The third critical task of the therapist is to model healthy communication/perception processes. He must be clear and specific in his interactions with the family and continually insist that they behave this way also. He should make sure that he understands what is being communicated by clarifying statements and feelings on a regular basis. At the same time, he can teach family members to display good perceptive behaviors by asking them to clarify others' statements and to give specific feedback to one another.

The three tasks outlined above are considered to be critical for a productive therapeutic relationship. They are somewhat antagonistic to one another in that the therapist is asked to behave in several potentially conflicting ways simultaneously. He is asked to be controlling yet accepting, and to be individually oriented yet concerned about the whole group. These may be behaviors that the family needs to develop, and, by demonstrating them from the beginning, the therapist can set the stage for later change. In other words, they are critical to the therapist in order to manage future sessions successfully, but they are also important to the family because they may be behaviors that will be required of them in order to function better in the future.

Observation and Assessment

The second stage in the process involves an analysis of each individual family. It is essentially an evaluation of specific and general dynamics that are present in each individual and in the unit. The therapist first attempts to identify and isolate specific problems that have propelled the family into therapy. These will be translated into short-term goals for the immediate future. Temporary resolution of the most pressing immediate concerns can free the family to deal with the more pervasive general dysfunction that is causing them pain. The long term goals relate specifically to this general dysfunction.

In order to be complete, this stage is of necessity multifaceted. Four phases can be identified, and each refers to a different yet related aspect of the family. One phase focuses on the immediate presenting problems. In the first session, short-term goals may be discussed and established that will deal directly with the most pressing problem. A second phase is the long range remediation of general dysfunction that may be present in members or in the entire unit. Another phase involves any evaluation of each family members' individual personality dynamics. The fourth phase is concerned with the dynamics of the unit as a whole. These phases are not isolated or progressive steps. They occur simultaneously and continuously in each session. They are only discrete entities in the mind of the therapist. They serve as a constant reminder of the complexity of the interactions that he is observing. They are different levels of involvement that all contribute to the dysfunctionality of the family. Each is essential for permanent change to occur and to be maintained.

The basis for observation and assessment are the five specific characteristics of families in the theory of personality. Using these concepts, the therapist develops a diagnostic picture of the entire unit. He can observe present interactions and evaluate past functioning based on this framework. An important element of this picture is the family's definition of their problem. How do they evaluate the past and present situations? How do they propose to resolve their difficulties?

The major portion of this stage can be accomplished in the first two or three sessions with a family. The primary dynamics should be observable in this period of time, and short- and long-term goals should be established by the end of the third session. This evaluation may then be shared with the family in a written or verbal manner. The family is then asked to react to the assessment and to the plans for future therapeutic contact.

The remaining three stages of therapy are based on this evaluation, and all therapeutic interventions will be guided by it. This is not to say that this therapeutic plan is unchangeable. Continual reevaluation of the working hypotheses is prudent and advisable. If changes are necessary, they should be discussed with the family and instituted immediately.

The general concept of observation and assessment may be summarized by the following:

a. Provides a diagnostic picture of individuals and of the unit.
b. Establishes short-term and long-range goals.
c. Determines present and future interventions.
d. Is flexible enough to incorporate new data as therapy progresses.
e. Can change based on the concept of continuous reevaluation.
f. Is shared with and accepted by the family and its individual members.

Intervention

Based on the diagnostic picture that was developed in the second stage, the therapist begins to actively intervene in the family system. Theoretically, intervention cannot occur until the evaluation has been completed. However, in reality, the therapist begins the change process from the first session. The behaviors that he uses to structure a family and to assess dynamics are intervention strategies. His mere presence, as a professional, causes the family to interact in a different way. This difference in family patterns can be pointed out and thus create change outside of the session. In other words, any contact that the therapist has with a family or any of its members is potentially an intervention.

However, we can identify more specific techniques that the counselor can use to institute change. The following are the major intervention strategies of the Integrative Family therapist.

THE DISCUSSION AND ENACTMENT OF SPECIFIC PROBLEM SITUATIONS. Using recent examples of conflict or immediate conflict situations, the therapist can provide a more objective analysis for the family and generate alternative solutions for its resolution. He can highlight critical incidents in the development and continuance of the problem. Frequently, this creates new insights for family members who then can see alternative ways of behaving. From time to time, the counselor may have to actively interpret the dynamics of the situation and suggest specific new behaviors. Whether the therapist is nondirectively guiding or actively manipulating a situation is dependent on the family's capacities. If the family is unable to creatively resolve a conflict with the indirect help of the therapist, he must become more active and directive. In other words, the behavior of the therapist is somewhat dictated by the needs and capabilities of each individual family. He must be prepared to function differently with each family or with the same family in different situations. In this way, he not only provides maximum assistance in specific situations but also models flexible problem-solving behaviors. He is telling the family verbally and nonverbally, directly and indirectly, that different situations require different responses. Flexibility is a key element in harmonious constructive growth.

USE OF CONFRONTATION TECHNIQUES TO HELP PEOPLE COMMUNICATE MORE ACCURATELY WITH ONE ANOTHER. Encourage all family members to discuss all aspects of a situation openly and directly. Discourage the continuance of hidden agendas and covert meanings in the communication/perception process. Encourage all members to speak openly about their perceptions and reactions. By reducing the threat of reprisal or retribution, the therapist creates an atmosphere of trust and honesty. When the threat is lowered, the need for protection and subterfuge is decreased.

USE OF COMMUNICATION CHECKS TO ENSURE ACCURATE PERCEPTION ON THE PART OF ALL FAMILY MEMBERS. Establish a pattern in the sessions of continually checking your perception of what has been communicated, and encourage family members to do the same. Assumptions and inaccurate perceptions should be immediately identified and corrected. The family can be instructed to practice these behaviors at home and to make them a permanent part of their interactional patterns. Checking one's perception is a learned behavior. The more practice a family receives, the more likely it is to continue that behavior in the future.

WORK OUT DEFINITE ROLES AND EXPECTATIONS FOR EACH MEMBER. Encourage all family members to identify specific expectations that they have for one another and specific tasks that are part of each other's roles. Individuals can negotiate aspects of their role in order to achieve mutually satisfying positions. Consequences may have to be established if tasks are not completed. The key element is mutuality. All members should feel that they have contributed to the establishment and maintenance of satisfying roles that are essential for the health of the unit.

HELP THE FAMILY TO SET RULES THAT WILL GOVERN THEIR DAILY INTERACTIONS. They can be very specific or general in nature. For example, family members should respect one another and listen to each other. More specific rules would include those concerning dating, having friends at the house, and curfew hours. It is up to the family to decide how they want to organize their daily living patterns. Rules can give them well-established guidelines for a smooth organization.

ENCOURAGE THE FAMILY TO HOLD REGULAR FAMILY MEETINGS TO SUPPLEMENT THE THERAPEUTIC CONTACTS. Meeting structure and content can be rehearsed and reviewed in the therapy sessions. Initially, they can be used to practice and reinforce the new behaviors learned in therapy. In the later stages of counseling, they will represent the major force for change in the future. They can eventually take the place of the therapeutic sessions.

The preceding six techniques are the primary strategies of the Integrative Family therapist. They are not the only therapeutic behaviors used. Each counselor must develop his own repertoire to supplement those presented here. No professional can be expected to fit any one predetermined therapeutic mold.

Change Maintenance

The primary task of the fourth stage of therapy is to reinforce new behaviors and patterns of interaction. The therapist may continue to use his intervention strategies, but probably in a less active, directive manner. The family is now taking more responsibility for their present and future behavior. The duration between sessions will begin to increase, and the therapist will gradually remove himself from a central position in the family. He can now help the family to generalize their new insights and behaviors to all aspects of their lives in and out of the unit. They are no longer focusing all of their energy on coping with present conflicts. A satisfying problem-solving process has emerged and is being used for the present and the future. The family is more optimistic about the future, and is actively involved in planning for it. However, the therapist must guard against moving too quickly through the fourth stage. Premature withdrawal of the therapist from an influential position in the unit can trigger the homeostatic mechanism. Without his continued input and reinforcement, a family can revert to old behavior patterns. Progressive movement through this fourth stage will decrease the likelihood of this occurring.

Review and Termination

Termination is indicated when a family is displaying the following behaviors:

a. Present-day conflicts are resolved in a mutually satisfying manner.

b. Members express optimism about future plans.
c. Family sets realistic long-term goals for the unit and for each individual member.
d. Each member has internalized the new behaviors, attitudes, and feelings.

When the therapist observes these behaviors occurring on a regular basis, he can plan for termination. He should first review the entire process for the family, and specifically reinforce the new behaviors and interactional patterns. He should then check each individual's feelings and attitudes toward the change that has occurred. Have they personalized and internalized the changes? Next, discuss the future goals of the unit and each member.

The final task of the therapist is to present written and oral feedback to the family concerning his perception of their therapeutic process. This would include the initial presenting problem, his assessment of the unit and each individual member's goals, a review of new individual and family behaviors, and an evaluation of their present functioning. It is suggested that this feedback be in written form as well as oral so that the family can review the therapist's evaluation at any time in the future. Families have told me that they review the feedback report at regular intervals during their family meetings. In this way, it provides continued reinforcement of therapy, long after formal counseling has ended.

As I previously stated, the stages in the therapeutic process are theoretical. They are part of the conceptual framework that is used to organize the therapy process, and to remediate dysfunctional families. The process itself is intensive and short-term. Most families complete the five stages in ten to twelve sessions. Some families can reach termination in as few as five sessions. Others require more extensive reorientation and may be in therapy for a year or more. Regardless of the duration, the theoretical process is essentially the same. Successful therapy, in other words, always involves the progressive movement from structuring to termination with all of the drama, pain, excitement, and pleasure of the intervening stages.

Key Words and Phrases

Two major goals of therapy
Structuring
First challenge of therapy
Observation and assessment
Intervention strategies
Change maintainance
Review and termination
Written feedback

CHAPTER 6

FAMILY THERAPY AND PSYCHOANALYSIS

LEONARD ELKUN, M.D.

DESCRIPTION OF MAJOR THEORIST

LEONARD D. ELKUN, M.D.

PROFESSIONAL POSITIONS. Private practice of Psychiatry and Psychoanalysis. Director of Psychiatric Services, Prairie House Addiction Research Center. Psychiatric Consultant, Department of Psychiatry, University of Chicago. Psychiatric Consultant, Circuit Court of Cook County, Illinois. Candidate, Chicago Institute for Psychoanalysis.

INTRODUCTION TO THEORY

UNTIL the late 1800s the treatment of "mentally disturbed" individuals primarily consisted of physical approaches. These were modalities directed more at the containment of disturbing behaviors than at the removal or cure of these problems in the suffering individuals. Treatment often consisted of sunshine, rest, wholesome food, hydrotherapy, exercise, soothing balms, and occasionally even physical tortures, intended to exorcise the mind of "devilish" ideas and feelings. The evolution of complex psychological therapies for treatment of disturbed individuals has been a major step forward in the development of a more humanistic, as well as a more therapeutically effective attitude toward mental illness. In addition, their emergence has also greatly enhanced our knowledge and understanding of normal and pathological mental functioning.

Late in the nineteenth century, psychoanalysis began as a mode of psychological therapy. Over the years it has come to represent significant theories of personality development and general psychological function and is currently the major representative of all the depth psychologies. The term *psycho-*

analysis refers exclusively to a mode of therapy that uses specialized techniques (such as Free Association) for the elaboration of unconscious psychical material, so that the complex meanings of the unconscious forces that motivate psychical life can be discovered and studied. While traditional psychoanalysis is still a very popular mode of therapy, it has undergone considerable shifts both in its theoretical range and in its clinical applicability since the time of the original theoretical documentation and writings of its founder, Sigmund Freud. At the present time, the insights and understandings that have been gained from an awareness and familiarity with psychoanalytic principles and techniques are primarily utilized by therapists practicing Psychoanalytically Oriented Psychotherapy. Because of certain changes in classical psychoanalytic technique, especially in the role assumed by the therapist and in the management of the inevitable Transferences that develop, psychoanalytically oriented psychotherapy has achieved a much greater acceptance in the broad field of treatment modalities.

THEORY OF PERSONALITY

Major Concepts

From the time of its first inception, the major thrust of psychoanalysis has been the acquisition of knowledge and understanding of unconscious psychical content and function. While there have been changes in certain basic psychoanalytic techniques and theory, the acquisition of insight into unconscious mental life has remained at the center of psychoanalytic thought and treatment. Psychoanalytic treatment is specifically geared to the task of gaining such insight so that restructuring of psychical functioning can occur where necessary.

A number of conceptualizations and hypotheses have been presented regarding the functioning of the mental apparatus. These hypotheses or "models of the mind" (such as the Topographic model, the Structural or Tripartite model, the Object Relations model, etc.) have been postulated in an attempt to clarify and organize the data of psychological functioning. In addition to the organization and structuring of this data, these constructions have been helpful in facilitating communication regarding psychoanalytic investigation and discovery. Despite the absence of a single all encompassing model of the mind, there have been a number of accepted basic assumptions regarding mental functioning. Psychoanalytic treatment has been based upon these assumptions. These assumptions include the following: the concept of the Unconscious; the concept of Psychic Determinism; the three Regulatory Principles of Mental Functioning (the Constancy Principle, the Pleasure Principle, and the Reality Principle); the concept of Intrapsychic Conflict; the concept of the Repetition Compulsion; the concept of Clinical Transference; and the concept of the Intrapsychic-Interpersonal Relationship.

The Unconscious

This concept assumes that there are significant aspects of mental functioning that occur out of the individual's conscious awareness, and that they are not readily available to consciousness by usual means such as through memory or focused attention. The Unconscious is believed to contain repressed memories of past events and painful affects as well as being the major site of conflict solution and resolution. It is important to note that the Unconscious does not represent a concrete organic "site" in the brain, but is only an intellectual construction that has proven very useful in organizing psychological data derived through the psychoanalytic framework.

Psychic Determinism

This concept assumes that all mental life has psychological meaning. That is, that all experience, whether cognitive, emotional, or action, is determined by activity from within the psychical apparatus. The origin of determined actions is within the unconscious mental life of an individual. This concept essentially rules out chance experiences, accidents, or any activity initiated through willpower or conscious choice.

Regulatory Principles of Mental Functioning

The mental apparatus is believed to operate "under the control" of several regulatory mechanisms of mental functioning. The goal of the regulatory mechanisms is to maintain homeostatic equilibrium within the system, such that psychical discomfort is avoided and psychical pleasure is attained. When tension, i.e. unconscious wishes, needs, desires, drives, and impulses, begins to accumulate in response to internal or external stimulation the psychical apparatus must adapt itself in such a way as to return the level of excitation within the total system to a homeostatic level. The regulatory mechanisms are the modes used by the psyche to deal with accumulated tension.

THE CONSTANCY PRINCIPLE. This principle is considered to be a significant cornerstone of Freudian psychoanalytic theory. The principle states that the psychical (mental) apparatus tends to keep the quality of excitation (tension) at as low a level and at as constant a level as possible. Constancy is achieved through the discharge or "abreaction" of increased energy, and by the avoidance via defense mechanisms of whatever might tend to increase the quantity of excitation.

THE PLEASURE PRINCIPLE. The essence of the pleasure principle is that the whole of psychical activity is aimed at avoiding unpleasure and procuring pleasure. The psychical apparatus is regulated by the avoidance or discharge of unpleasurable tension. Thus the Principle of Constancy is closely allied with the Pleasure Principle in that unpleasure is seen as a subjective perception of an increase in tension, and the perception of pleasure corresponds to a decrease in tension.

THE REALITY PRINCIPLE. This principle is closely coupled with the Pleasure Principle, which it modifies. In so far as it succeeds in establishing its dominance as a regulatory principle of mental functioning, it guides the search for the discharge of unpleasurable tension through an indirect route of "detours and postponements of direct discharge" according to the conditions imposed by the outside world. More simply stated, the Reality Principle regulates the patterns of tension discharge in a realistic acceptable way.

Intrapsychic Conflict

Psychoanalysis uses the term "conflict" to represent a situation of contradictory internal requirements opposed to each other within the individual. For example, a conflict may be between a wish and a moral imperative, between two contradictory emotions, or it may be expressed in more distorted fashion such as in the formation of neurotic symptoms, troubled behavioral actions, or character disturbances. It is felt that intrapsychic conflict is a constitutive part of the individual and that resolution of conflict is crucial in the development of the personality and in the daily life of psychical function ing.

Repetition Compulsion

The Repetition Compulsion is an automatic, innate process that unconsciously forces the individual to repeat a conflictual dynamic over and over. More recently, the goal of the Repetition Compulsion has been felt to be reflective of a Drive towards Mastery. In effect then, the Repetition Compulsion operates concretely such that an individual will repeatedly seek out circumstances that place him in the distressing conflict situation, thereby repeating an old experience with the wish to master the formerly less well-mastered conflict on this occassion. Because the individual utilizes the same unsuccessful methods of conflict solution as he formerly did, mastery continues to be elusive, forcing yet further continuing repetitions. This concept is extremely important in the theory of psychoanalytically oriented treatment.

Clinical Transference

The concept of Transference is a central factor in psychoanalytic theory and clinical practice. Clinical Transference refers exclusively to the mode of reemergence of archaic conflicts and affects within the therapeutic relationship. Simply stated, the patient "transfers" (or projects) onto the person of the therapist his unconscious (repressed) archaic wishes and expectations and reexperiences these projected conflicts with intense affect and fantasy. The development of the Clinical Transference and its vicissitudes provides the major avenue for the exploration of unconscious content and function. It is within the Transference relationship that the basic problems of an analysis "play themselves out." The establishment, the nature, the interpretation, and the eventual resolution of Transference issues are in fact what ultimately defines the "cure." Thus, in traditional psychoanalytic therapy, the analysis of the "Transference Neurosis," i.e. the total configuration of transferences onto the therapist, is at the center of the therapeutic task and therapeutic process. The establishment of Transference is one important example of the Repetition Compulsion in action.

Intrapsychic-Interpersonal Relationship

A basic concept of psychoanalytic understanding and treatment is that conflict is contained within the individual psychical apparatus. The stimulus for an intrapsychic conflict may often arise from an external source, such as an interpersonal "conflict." But the major focus of attention of psychoanalytic investigation is upon the intrapsychic functioning of the individual and his capacities to resolve intrapsychic conflicts. The external world, especially interpersonal involvements, often provides the forum for the staging of typical intrapsychical conflict and solution.

Personality Development

It is felt that as the young child develops and is forced to psychologically confront different and phase-appropriate internal and external conflict situations in his life structuralized enduring patterns of conflict solution will be "laid down." These well-established, mostly unconscious patterns of conflict solution become the major and "characteristic" personality traits of the individual. In other words, with time and repeated experience the individual will unconsciously solve conflict situations in similar, predictable ways. This characteristic of repetitiousness is valid whether conflict situations are solved in adaptive or maladaptive fashion. Thus the "character makeup" of an individual is a direct reference to his idiosyncratic and predictable patterns of solving inner drive tension states. Whether the eventual characterologic (personality) formations of an individual are functional or not, they are always subjectively in harmony (or syntonic) with his sense of self. Because the character structure is so familiar and reliable to the person, it rarely causes him conscious difficulty. Only when certain conditions occur, which will be further elaborated, does the personality structure become dystonic to the individual. In psychoanalytically oriented treatment, the major focus of attention becomes the psyche's effectiveness in regulating inner drive tensions, and in restructuring areas of "defective" regulation within the characterologic makeup of the patient.

Early in psychoanalytic history, "normal" mental functioning was loosely defined by Freud as "the capacity to achieve and be productive in work, and to enjoy social interactions." These ideas have now been significantly broadened and have a more directly intrapsychic focus of evaluation. It is now felt that "effective" psychical functioning is reflected in the capacity of an individual to maintain homeostatic equilibrium in the following areas:

1. Tension regulation
2. The pursuit and achievement of neutralized goals and ideals
3. Regulation and maintenance of self-esteem
4. Mutuality in relationships

Tension Regulation

A well-functioning personality reflects the capacity to maintain homeostasis under a variety of situations. This is achieved by the discharge of inner tension when there is a buildup and by avoidance of conflict situations that create overwhelming excitation within the psychical apparatus. Significantly, this capacity to regulate tension does not eliminate the experiencing of intense affects (such as pain, sexuality, sadness, euphoria, etc.) impassioned ideas, etc.. It does not require a "dull, monotoned" existence for homeostasis. The individual is flexible and can adjust to a whole range of internal tensions and affects.

Goals and Ideals

The well-functioning personality ideally has a structured yet flexible realistically determined set of personal standards and goals to strive for. He must also have an active energetic motivational component to his personality that allows him to consistently pursue these standards and goals. In addition to the motivation to pursue realistic goals and standards, the goals themselves must yield pleasurable reward in their achievement (unlike, for example, the antisocial "criminal" personality types). The establishment of enduring, realistically determined, pleasure yielding goals and ideals is absolutely dependent on the developing child's having been supportively nurtured in an atmosphere of optimal frustration. That is, the environment was such that it allowed the young child to be unsuccessful without undue trauma or disappointment and successful without inappropriately excessive praise. Such an environment facilitates a slow step by step "laying down" of realistic attainable goals, as well as the establishment of the capacity to energetically pursue goals without fear of precipitous emotional imbalance.

Regulation of Self-esteem

A very significant factor in "normal" psychical functioning is the maintenance and regulation of a well-balanced sense of self and self-esteem. An important aspect of the sense of self is the capacity for independent self-determined functioning. A cohesive sense of self and a homeostatic level of self-esteem are reflected in the capacity of an individual to exhibit himself and his capabilities in a realistic manner and in accordance with his own realistically established goals and ideals. It is very common for difficulties in the regulation of self-esteem to bring individuals to therapy. Swings in the levels of self-esteem cause people their greatest satisfactions in life as well as their greatest disappointments and pain. A normally functioning personality is able to deal with great pleasure and great disappointment without feelings of disintegration or diminution in the cohesive sense of self.

Mutuality and Group Function

An important indicator of effective psychical functioning is the capacity for mutuality in relationships. This capacity refers to the ability of an individual to engage in a mutually enjoyable, intimate relationship with another individual or group of individuals. It includes the aspects of sharing of emotional states (for example sexuality, sadness, euphoria, etc.) with empathy and understanding as well as the capacity to cooperate in mutually gratifying, externally directed activites. The ability of an individual to function successfully in a group, e.g. the family, a professional group, a social group, is reflective of a well-established sense of self and independent identity. It requires strength and flexibility to transiently sacrifice individual goals and satisfactions, where necessary, for the sake of effective group functioning and the satisfaction of group goals. Dysfunction in this area is another prime mover in bringing individuals for psychotherapeutic intervention.

Psychopathology

Psychopathological formations and behaviors occur as a result of an "overload" mental apparatus and its subsequent incapacity to "handle" excess tension in its usual and characterologic manner. Thus when the psyche is "traumatized," i.e. overwhelmed with excess affect or tension that cannot be effectively discharged via usual modes of discharge, it must seek the reestablishment of homeostasis in the most competent and economical means at its disposal. Psychological symptoms such as Acute Anxiety States, Depression, Hypochondriasis, Phobias, Compulsive Rituals, Hysterical Conversion Reactions, etc., offer the psyche ready discharge routes. Symptom formation allows for partial discharge of blocked tension and also allows the psyche to "put out of its awareness" or repress the formerly unresolvable conflicts and their attendant affects (such as anger, guilt, shame, anxiety, sadness). This results in an acute removal of disturbing tension buildup. While these new, although pathological resolutions do offer relief from dammed up affect and tension, at the same time they impair the formerly uninhibited functioning of the character structure. The existence of a psychological symptom is experienced as a "foreign body" (or a dystonic formation) that the personality must incorporate and begin to "work with."

It is important to note that while there are well-known and familiar secondary gain aspects to symptoms, the primary gain of any and all symptoms is the binding of excess unpleasurable tension and the rapid restoration of homeostasis. Thus when a process of symptom formation has occurred we can assume that there has been some unresolvable conflict between inner drive tension (Pleasure Principle) and some aspect of Reality (Reality Principle) that has resulted in blocked discharge of tension. Because of their effectiveness in restoring homeostasis to a traumatized psychical apparatus, symptoms are given up with great difficulty. To do so forces the individual to reexperience the formerly overwhelming and very painful tensions and affects. While symptoms are very often within the patient's conscious awareness, the etiologic roots are never conscious. This then becomes a major goal of treatment, namely the uncovering of the unconscious bases and etiologic factors in symptom formation.

The essential issue in psychopathological formations, therefore, is the psyche's ineffectual reactions to acute or chronically stressful situations. The source of the homeostatic imbalance may be either related to a specific stress or related to the state of the personality at the time of a particular stress. In other words, an overwhelming stress situation such as the death of a parent or child, the loss of a limb, an acute and severe loss of self-esteem, etc., can tumble an otherwise well-functioning personality into transient symptom formation. On the other hand, a fairly insignificant stress situation befalling an already beleaguered, partially overwhelmed mental apparatus can initiate the process of symptom formation. It is often very difficult to specifically determine the events that lead to an acute outbreak of neurotic symptom formation, unless the external stress is one of great magnitude, such as the death of a parent or child. In either case the problem rests in the management of the tension within the psyche.

Whatever factor may precipitate neurotic illness, the area that must be eventually approached in the treatment is an analysis of the mental apparatus' ability to manage tension. Ultimately changes and restructuralizations must be made where defects exist in this capacity. It is important to establish that it is not only major life-disrupting events that can precipitate neurotic outbreaks. Many stresses of daily living, such as struggles in self-esteem, achievement, relations with others, etc., can bring on neurotic illness, especially when they encounter an already anxiety-ridden character structure.

All behaviors, whether verbal, cognitive, or action, reflect unconsciously determined conflicts and their resolutions. Thus distorted dysfunctional behavior, as well as internal tension disequilibrium, reflect maladaptive conflict solving patterns. It is relevant to note that the psychoanalytic therapist approaches symptoms and external dysfunctional behaviors as guide posts that direct one's attentions to unconsciously located disturbed conflict solutions rather than as primary targets for therapeutic intervention and removal. As treatment progresses, however, and the underlying conflict solving patterns become more and more resolved, symptomatic behaviors recede and are replaced by more adaptive functional activity.

Key Words and Phrases

Psychoanalysis
Psychoanalytically oriented psychotherapy
Models of the mind
Unconscious
Psychic determinism
Regulatory principles of mental functioning
Homeostasis
Abreaction
Unpleasure-pleasure
Conflict
Repetition compulsion

Transference
Transference neurosis

Personality traits
Optimal frustration
Sense of self
Self-esteem

Mutuality
Psychical trauma
Symptom formation
Primary gain
Secondary gain

THERAPEUTIC PROCESS

Theory of Therapy

As noted previously a basic assumption of psychoanalytic theory is that long established psychical structure, whether adaptive or symptom producing, will persist and endure endlessly. Based on the concept of the Repetition Compulsion, these unconscious patterns will repeat and repeat. In the case of symptomatic anxiety-based behaviors these repetitions will continue to produce similar predictable discomfort and inhibition of action unless the unconscious roots of these patterns are made conscious and ultimately analyzed. One of the initial goals of psychoanalytic treatment is the establishment of a therapeutic milieu. This environment will facilitate the reemergence and reexperiencing of archaic infantile conflict and their solutions within the therapy setting. The reemergence of archaic conflicts occurs mainly through the development of the Clinical Transference projected onto the therapist. The unfolding transference becomes the bulk of what is to be analyzed during treatment. The major aim is for these earliest, ofttimes dysfunctional conflict solutions to be examined and eventually restructured. While symptomatic relief is sought in therapy, the aspects of reconstruction and restructuralization of the personality, i.e. the conflict-solving capacities, assume the primary focus of attention. Simply stated, careful repeated examination of how one struggled with an eventually solved problem in the archaic past (often under situations of stress, and with an infantile psychical apparatus) will gradually lead to a greater and greater capacity to struggle with and eventually resolve problems in the present with increasing effectiveness. This result is primarily related to the reexamination of past (archaic) problems as they emerge in the Clinical Transference. But now they are looked at in a modulated supportive environment and with the observing capacity of a more mature, more flexible, less stressed psychical apparatus in the patient.

A very significant factor in psychoanalytic treatment is the process of *working through.* This concept refers to the repeated presentation in the treatment setting of conflict solution and to the process by which these solution patterns are slowly altered. Repeated clarification and interpretation of the unconscious roots of conflict situations and the vicissitudes of particular solution patterns as they occur repeatedly in the therapy induces a gradual transformation. The psyche begins to make more and more adaptive, homeostatic resolutions. This is the way in which old dysfunctional patterns are slowly and gradually altered in the direction of more functional adaptive patterns of conflict solution.

However, of extreme importance is that the clarification and interpretation of these patterns be connected with the discharge of long repressed, associated memories and affects (such as anger, depression, anxiety, shame, guilt, etc.) that are directly related to the conflict situations being interpreted. For example, a patient may come to an understanding of the vicissitudes of a particular conflict situation that led to extreme feelings of shame, but if during the analysis of this conflict he does not also reexperience the intense feelings of shame that were associated with the original conflict situation, then restructuralization of conflict-solving patterns will be incomplete. In other words, a cognitive awareness of dysfunctional patterns is not by itself therapeutic. It is the combination of a clarified conflict and the "abreacted" associated affects and memories from the past that is the essence of what is therapeutic. One of the very common resistances to progress in treatment occurs when the individual becomes intellectually aware of his struggles, i.e. they are cognitive and conscious to him, but without the recognition and reexperiencing of the associated affects. One then sees a "well-versed" but incompletely treated individual whose basic patterns have not been adequately restructured.

Role of the Therapist

Very simply stated, the initial role of the therapist is to bring what is out of the individual's awareness (unconscious) into his conscious awareness. This includes present conflicts, their associated affects and memories, and the relationships between present and past similar conflict situations and their solutions. The therapist provides a central figure or "Transference Object" around whom archaic conflictual struggles are reenacted, reexperienced, and eventually resolved. As part of the therapeutic relationship, it is an important responsibility of the therapist to help create an atmosphere in which the patient can comfortably and with a feeling of support allow himself to reexperience his archaic, pain-studded past. The therapist and the patient both contribute to the establishment and maintenance of an adequate therapeutic milieu and therapeutic alliance. The patient must come to the treatment with a sense of "basic trust," i.e. with enough positive, enriching past experience with significant "helping" persons (for example with parents, teachers, clergy, doctors, etc.) that allows him to commit himself to an in-depth involvement with another human being and to have the firm expectation that this person basically wishes him well and wishes to be helpful to him. The therapist must have capacity for empathy with the struggles of the patient and a willingness to participate with the patient in an even-handed, nonjudgmental, consistent, and supportive way, as the individual attempts to resolve his life conflicts.

While therapy cannot proceed without this basic alliance and therapeutic milieu, the primary role of the therapist remains in his analytic function. Thus the therapist exercises his major role in his attempts at interruption of long established, dysfunctional psychical patterns of operation through repeated clarification, elaboration, and interpretation of the precipitants and variables of past and current conflict solution. An important principle of psychoanalytic interpretation is that the therapist's interventions are always intended to facilitate the patient's making new and more adaptive solutions to his conflictual struggles. However these new solutions (resolutions) must always be idiosyncratic to his personality and in accordance with his own established goals and ideals. Gross identifications with the therapist's patterns of problem solving will not enhance the process of growth and individuation, but in fact, may hamper the emergence of a free, individualized, and idealized psychical apparatus.

Initially however, patients often make important identifications with the therapist. This occurs particularly in that the therapist provides an initial role model as a "curious" other, interested in struggling with the patient's dysfunctions. The therapist's lack of fear in confronting troubling issues within the patient and his approach to problems with an accepting nonjudgmental attitude will encourage the patient to do the same. The patient will be stimulated to heighten his curiosity about himself and to increase his wish to struggle more effectively with his problems. As therapy progresses, the analyzing function of the therapist is increasingly taken over by the patient, resulting in the establishment of an important, enduring, self-observing, and self-analyzing capacity.

Phases of Treatment

The progression of therapy can be divided into three fairly distinct phases: the opening phase, the middle phase, and the termination phase. The following are the essential elements that comprise the *opening phase*: the development of the therapeutic alliance, the establishment of a therapeutic milieu, the early emergence of clinical transference reactions, and the beginning unfolding of a significant psychological history. This includes for example, the history of the current illness as well as any other past psychological illnesses. In general, the opening phase is highlighted by a gradual emergence and description of the life style and the conflict-solving patterns of the individual. The therapy begins heading in the direction of specific foci of homeostatic vulnerabilities.

The *middle phase* is comprised mainly of the analysis of conflict. The major work of this phase is in the slow, gradual resolving of reemerged archaic conflicts, and the restructuralization of the psychical apparatus, particularly where there has been weakness or defect. The major therapeutic tools of this stage are clarification, explication, and interpretation. During this phase of therapy the therapist is often presented with the patient's greatest internal resistances to change. However an even-handed consistent interpretive stance will eventually allow defensive resistances to drop away. With the analysis of resistance, the therapeutic process continues. It is during this phase that the process of working through is repeatedly encountered. The "work" of analyzing is in the repeated interpretation of the conflictual forces and counterforces and how they have led to particular patterns of conflict solution in the past and currently. As "insight" is gained into the unconscious roots and variables of specific conflict solutions, only then do new and more adaptive resolutions begin to occur and be "laid down."

The *termination phase* of therapy begins when certain criteria of functioning are increasingly achieved. The main indication for the onset of the termination phase is the gradual resolution of the transference relationship and its vicissitudes (the "Transference Neurosis"). As restructuralization of the psychical apparatus proceeds, the individual will reflect a greatly heightened capacity for handling formerly anxiety-producing situations without trauma or symptomatic formations. He will reveal a generalized decrease in uncontrolled tension states, and a greater flexibility and resilience in the total personality. These changes will also result in a noticeable heightened capacity for humor, wisdom, and a sense of cosmic proportion, i.e. the ability to realistically evaluate one's place in one's world.

In addition to specific external behavioral changes such as more successful and gratifying interpersonal relationships, the individual will unfold a life style in much closer accordance with his own now realistically determined goals and standards. As a result, the levels of self-esteem will be increasingly homeostatic and enduring. The individual will also show a greater capacity to effectively deal with disappointment, excitement, and other formerly disruptive affects. Freeing-up of unconscious affect, unconscious fantasy, e.g. dreams, daydreams, and increased access to unconscious contents and ideas will be obvious.

An important indicator of imminent termination is a well-established self-analyzing capacity that ensures ongoing self-analysis and understanding long after formal treatment ends. The self-analytic capacity will allow the individual to harmoniously confront new life stresses as well as to continue working through his past life stresses as they are inevitably restimulated. The termination phase often includes a mild reemergence of earlier stressful anxieties, particularly towards the end of treatment. This is precipitated by the impending separation from the therapist and the milieu. However these anxieties recede following the termination of therapy.

Key Words and Phrases

Therapeutic milieu
Therapeutic alliance
Working through
Transference object
Empathy
Interpretation
Resolution of conflict
Restructralization
Self-analyzing capacity

PSYCHOANALYSIS AND FAMILY TREATMENT

The conceptual transition between psychoanalytically based individual therapy and family treatment modalities seems at times difficult to negotiate. However, they both have similar goals, namely the relief of human suffering and the attempt to understand vulnerabilities and make repair where possible. It is common to both modalities to assume that recurrence of disruptive symptoms (repetition compulsion) can absolutely be expected without therapeutic intervention. While the therapeutic goals are similar, there are certain similarities and differences in therapeutic approach that are important to elaborate and clarify.

As previously stated, the major focus of the psychoanalytically oriented therapist's interventions is on the intrapsychic system, whereas in the Family Treatment model the focus of therapeutic intervention is on the Supraindividual system. The individual therapist attempts to view the inner experiences of the patient in conflict through the process of introspection and empathy. The family therapist must focus on both the inner experience of each member of a family group as well as upon the complex transactional aspects between group members. The individual therapist focuses on the unconscious intrapsychic "response system" that is initiated in reaction to a wide range of external and internal stimuli. Comparatively, the family therapist often focuses on the environmental stimuli (most often the other group members themselves) that unconsciously initiate group reaction. While the foci of these two therapeutic modalities appear quite different, there are theoretical gaps that can be bridged. Namely that what is therapeutic for both systems of treatment is the alteration in the structuralized reactive patterns of the individual psychical system (in individual therapy) and of the family interactional system (in family therapy).

Like all groups, families have dynamics (forces and counterforces) that result either in functional or dysfunctional conflict solutions. Families with consistently dysfunctional problem-solving capacities will come to treatment because of chronic, painful disequilibrium. Where homeostasis is maintained, however, families will frequently not come to treatment. This is often true, even if the homeostasis is maintained at the expense of the individuation and growth of one or more of the group members. Thus, as is seen with the individual seeking therapy, families will turn for therapeutic intervention only when all attempts at maintaining homeostasis within the system fail. Similar to the stresses that precipitate symptom formation in individuals, families become "symptomatic" or "dystonic" when the system becomes overloaded and overwhelmed with tension that cannot be adequately handled.

In a family treatment setting, the therapist is involved with the total family system and its interactional patterns. But he cannot lose sight of the individual needs and demands of each member of the group. A significant commonality between psychoanalytic treatment and family treatment that must be kept in mind is the nature of the personality that each individual family member brings to the total family interactional arena. For example, individuals with disturbed intrapsychic states will by necessity continually turn to the family with the hope of satisfaction and repair of past hurts. Therefore, the family therapist must be in empathic touch with the individual needs of all group members in order to appreciate the underlying, often unspoken, unclear motives and "missions" within the family's interactional patterns. Attention only to the "superficial" interactional activity, may allow deeper, more complex psychological conflicts and configurations to remain hidden and untreated.

Thus, the dual goal of the family therapist is to enhance the effectiveness of functioning in the total family system, but at the same time trying to enhance the growth, development, and individuation of each family member as well. This can occasionally give rise to conflict especially at times in which the goals of the group may directly conflict with the individual goals of a particular group member. However, while effective group (family) functioning may occasionally delimit individual expression, it also provides important compensatory sources of security, support, and enhancement of self-esteem. The family can provide opportunities to fulfill both individual and group needs, such as parental roles, marital roles, teaching roles, etc.. The successful fulfillment of these roles will yield an internal sense of harmony and heightened self-esteem, both within the individual and within the total family group.

As in individual therapy, conflict-solving patterns in the family will only be altered and the alterations endure when the unknown unconscious patterns are made conscious along with the recognition and discharge of associated repressed affects and memories. A process very much like that of working through is seen in effective family treatment wherein conflicts and stress situations that arise during the course of therapy will be repeatedly confronted, clarified, and interpreted. The conflicts and their solutions are always elaborated and interpreted with the intent of making clear to all family members how the problem-solving system operates and repeats endlessly unless interrupted through "insight" into the system. In addition, how particular resolutions affect each member needs to be clearly elaborated. This process facilitates a slow, step by step modification in the problem-solving capacities of the whole family and eventually leads to more homeostatic effective family functioning. In addition, a "reconstructive dialogue" is created in family therapy, through a process of interruption, clarification, and interpretation of old interactional patterns and their previously unknown and misunderstood determinants. This "dialogue" is aimed at the development of mutual understanding and reconciliation within the family. Thus, the essential therapeutic agent in individual psychoanalytically oriented treatment and in family therapy is the interruption and alteration of old maladaptive patterns of problem solving, and the restructuralization into more adaptive, tension reducing satisfaction-producing patterns of functioning.

Family treatment begins drawing to a close when certain criteria of functioning are met, both within the group setting and for each member on an individual basis. The group must now be able to function in accord with realistic group goals, the achievement of which should now enhance the self-esteem and homeostatic balance of all group members. In addition, group functioning should not impose serious restriction in individual expression in order to achieve group homeostasis. Termination of family therapy is imminent when new solution (resolution) patterns are established — reflected mainly by the capacity to handle formerly stressful stimuli with ease and efficiency. Therefore, similar to the termination phase of individual therapy, families approaching termination will show a greater flexibility and resilience in "personality" as well as a greater capacity for maintaining levels of interactional harmony. As in individual therapy, effective family therapy results in the acquisition by the family of the capacity to continue "analysis" of its conflicts as they inevitably arise in the future (self-analyzing capacity).

Key Words and Phrases

Supraindividual system
Family interactional system
Reconstructive dialogue

BIBLIOGRAPHY

Ackerman, Nathan: *Family Process.* New York, Basic, 1970.

Ackerman, Nathan: *Treating the Troubled Family.* New York, Basic, 1966.

Ackerman, Nathan, Loeb, J., and Pierce, J.K.: *Family Therapy in Transition.* New York, Little, 1970.

Dodson, Laura and Kurpius, D.: *Family Counseling: A Systems Approach.* Muncie, Accelerated Development, 1977.

Erickson, Gerald and Terrence Hogan: *Family Therapy.* Monterey, Brooks-Cole, 1972.

Ferber, Andrew, et al.: *The Book of Family Therapy.* Boston, HM, 1972.

Foley, Vincent: *An Introduction to Family Therapy.* New York, Grune, 1974.

Gordon, Thomas: *Parent Effectiveness Training.* New York, P. H. Wyden, 1970.

Guerin, Philip: *Family Therapy.* New York, Wiley, 1976.

Haley, Jay: *Changing Families.* New York, Grune, 1971.

Haley, Jay: *Problem-Solving Therapy.* San Francisco, Jossey-Bass, 1976.

Haley, Jay, and Hoffman, Lynn: *Techniques of Family Therapy.* New York, Basic, 1967.

Hardy, Richard and Cull, J.: *Therapeutic Needs of the Family.* Springfield, Thomas, 1974.

Jackson, Donald: *Communication, Family, and Marriage.* Palo Alto, Sci & Behavior, 1968.

Kantor, David and Lehr, William: *Inside the Family.* San Francisco, Jossey-Bass, 1975.

Langaley, Donald and Kapla, David: *The Treatment of Families in Crisis.* New York, Grune, 1968.

Lewis, Jerry M.: *No Single Thread: Psychological Health in Family Systems.* New York, Brunner-Mazel, 1976.

Luthman, Shirley, and Kirschenbaum, M.: *The Dynamic Family.* Palo Alto, Sci & Behavior, 1974.

MacGregor, Robert, et al.: *Multiple Impact Therapy with Families.* New York, McGraw, 1964.

Minuchin, Salvador: *Families & Family Therapy.* Cambridge, Harvard, 1974.

Minuchin, Salvador, et al.: *Families of the Slums.* New York, Basic, 1967.

Napier, Augustus and Witaker, Carl: *The Family Crucible.* New York, Har-Row, 1978.

Olson, David: *Treating Relationships.* Lake Mills, Graphic, 1976.

Papp, Peggy: *Family Therapy, Full Length Case Studies.* New York, Wiley, 1977.

Patterson, Gerald: *Families* 2nd ed. Champaign, Res Press, 1975.
Patterson, Gerald: *Living with Children* 3rd ed. Champaign, Res Press, 1976.
Richter, Horst: *The Family as Patient.* New York, Farrar, Straus, and Giroux, 1970.
Satir, Virginia: *Conjoint Family Therapy.* Palo Alto, Sci & Behavior, 1967.
Satir, Virginia: *Peoplemaking.* Palo Alto, Sci & Behavior, 1972.
Skynner, A. C.: *Systems of Family and Marital Psychotherapy.* New York, Brunner-Mazel, 1976.
Thorman, George: *Family Therapy: A Handbook.* Beverly Hills, Western Psych, 1965.
Zuk, Gerald: *Family Therapy.* New York, Behavioral Pubns, 1971.

INDEX

T

U

W

Z